THE TEMPLE OF SOLOMON

AMERICAN ACADEMY OF RELIGION
SOCIETY OF BIBLICAL LITERATURE
RELIGION AND THE ARTS

Edited by

Anthony Yu

and

Joseph Gutmann

Number 3

THE TEMPLE OF SOLOMON

Archaeological Fact and Medieval Tradition
in Christian, Islamic and Jewish Art

Edited by

Joseph Gutmann

SCHOLARS PRESS
Missoula, Montana

THE TEMPLE OF SOLOMON

Archaeological Fact and Medieval Tradition
in Christian, Islamic and Jewish Art

Edited by

Joseph Gutmann

Published by

SCHOLARS PRESS

for

The American Academy of
Religion
and
The Society of Biblical
Literature

Distributed by

SCHOLARS PRESS
University of Montana
Missoula, Montana 59801

THE TEMPLE OF SOLOMON

Archaeological Fact and Medieval Tradition
in Christian, Islamic and Jewish Art

Edited by

Joseph Gutmann

Copyright © 1976

The American Academy of Religion
and
The Society of Biblical Literature

Library of Congress Cataloging in Publication Data

The Temple of Solomon

   (Religion and the arts ; 3)
   Papers read at the annual meeting of the Society
of Biblical Literature held in Chicago, Nov. 9,
1973.
   Bibliography: p.
   Includes index.
   1. Jerusalem. Temple. 2. Art, Medieval—
Addresses, essays, lectures. 3. Illumination of
books and manuscripts, Jewish—Spain—Addresses,
essays, lectures. I. Gutmann, Joseph. II. Society
of Biblical Literature. III. Series.
N5975.T45   726'.3   75-19120
ISBN 0-89130-013-9

Printed in the United States of America

Edwards Brothers, Inc.
Ann Arbor, Michigan 48104

CONTENTS

List of Illustrations	vi
Preface	xi
The Basic Structure of Solomon's Temple and Archaeological Research *Jean Ouellette*	1
The Temple of Solomon in Early Christian and Byzantine Art *Stanley Ferber*	21
Solomonic Elements in Romanesque Art *Walter Cahn*	45
The Temple of Solomon in Islamic Legend and Art *Priscilla Soucek*	73
The Messianic Temple in Spanish Medieval Hebrew Manuscripts *Joseph Gutmann*	125
Contributors	146
Selected Bibliography	147
Index	150
Illustrations	159

LIST OF ILLUSTRATIONS*

1. Plan of palace and temple at Tell Tainat.   161
2. Plan of Iron Age temple at Tell Arad.   162
3. Plan of temple at Hazor (Stratum Ib).   163
4. Pottery model of small temple from Idalion, Cyprus.   164
5. Plan of a *ḫilâni* at Zinçirli.   165
6. Layard's drawing of Assyrian relief from Kouyunjik.   166
7. "Trojans attacking a walled camp," Milan Iliad, Milan, Bibl. Ambrosiana, Cod. F. 205 Inf.   167
8. "Bethlehem," Mosaic on Triumphal arch, S. Maria Maggiore, Rome.   168
9. "Life of Solomon and building the Temple," Bible of San Pedro of Roda, Paris, Bibl. Nationale, lat. Ms. 6, fol. 129v.   169
10. "Temple in the Wilderness," Codex Amiatinus, Florence, Bibl. Laurentiana, Amiatinus 1, fols. 2v-3.   170

LIST OF ILLUSTRATIONS VII

11. "Tabernacle," First Leningrad Bible,
    Leningrad, Public Library, Ms. II, 17.   171
12. Torah case, Samaritan, Samaritan
    Temple Treasure, Nablus.   172
13. "Tabernacle/Temple," Samaritan
    drawing, location unknown.   173
14. Illustration to Psalm 113,
    Mt. Athos Psalter, Mt. Athos, Ms.
    Patocrator 61, fol. 165.   174
15. Harām al-Sharīf (Temple precinct),
    Jerusalem.   175
16. "Map of Jerusalem," London, British
    Museum, Add. 32343, fol. 15.   176
17. "*Iachim* and *Booz*," formerly facade,
    Würzburg Cathedral.   177
18. Fragment of a knotted column,
    Darmstadt, Hessisches Landesmuseum.   178
19. Fragment of a knotted column, Darmstadt,
    Hessisches Landesmuseum.   179
20. Central portal of the west facade,
    Ferrara Cathedral.   180
21. "David as a shepherd," Paris Psalter,
    Paris, Bibl. Nationale, Ms. gr. 139,
    fol. 1v.   181

LIST OF ILLUSTRATIONS

22. "Ascension," Homilies of James
of Kokkinobaphos, Paris, Bibl. Nationale,
Ms. gr. 1208, fol. 3v. 182

23. Niche, Dome of the Rock, Jerusalem
(left). Tomb of Baldwin V, after a drawing
of Elzear Horn (right). 183

24. South portal of west facade,
St. Lazare, Avallon. 184

25. "Bukhtnaṣṣar orders the destruction of
the Temple," Al-Bīrūnī, *Āthār al-Bāqiya*,
Edinburgh University Library,
Ms. No. 161, fol. 134v. 185

26. "Solomon deludes the demons into finishing
the Temple," Rashīd al-Dīn, *Jāmi'
al-Tawārīkh*, Istanbul,
Topkapi Sarayi Müzesi Kütüphanesi,
Hazine 1654, fol. 18v. 186

27. Sketch plan of Harām al-Sharīf
with Dome of the Rock and
Masjid al-Aqṣā. 187

28. Tree with jeweled trunk from a
pier of the octagonal arcade, Dome of the
Rock, Jerusalem. 188

29. Composite plant with jeweled ornaments
from a pier of the octagonal arcade,
Dome of the Rock, Jerusalem. 189

LIST OF ILLUSTRATIONS   IX

30. Plants hung with crowns and jewels,
    inner surface of octagonal arcade,
    Dome of the Rock, Jerusalem.   190

31. "The Prophet Muhammad leads other
    Prophets in prayer on his visit to Masjid
    al-Aqṣā," *Mi'rāj Nāmeh*, Paris, Bibl.
    Nationale, Suppl. turc 190, fol. 7.   191

32. "The Prophet Muhammad chooses milk
    in Masjid al Aqṣā," Istanbul, Topkapi
    Sarayi Müzesi Kütüphanesi,
    Hazine 2154, fol. 62.   192

33. "The Prophet's vision of Masjid al-Aqṣā
    during the discussion with Abū Bakr,"
    Istanbul, Topkapi Sarayi Müzesi
    Kütüphanesi, Hazine 2154, fol. 107.   193

34. "Sanctuary vessels," Bible, Paris, Bibl.
    Nationale, Ms. hebr. 7, fol. 12v.   194

35. "Sanctuary vessels," Bible, Paris, Bibl.
    Nationale, Ms. hebr. 7, fol. 13.   195

36. Handwashing device, al-Jazarī, *Treatise on
    Automata*, Washington, Freer Gallery of
    Art, Acc. No. 30.75.   196

37. "Sanctuary vessels," Pentateuch, Istanbul,
    Karaite synagogue, p. 18.   197

LIST OF ILLUSTRATIONS

38. "Sanctuary vessels," Pentateuch, Istanbul, Karaite synagogue, p. 19.   197
39. "Mount of Olives," Bible, Paris, Bibl. Nationale, Ms. hebr. 31, fol. 4.   198

We wish to express our gratitude to the following individuals and institutions for their aid and permission to reproduce the photographs: Cover photo, Prof. Paul L. Garber, Howland-Garber Model Reconstruction of Solomon's Temple; fig. 9, Prof. John Williams; 10, Florence, Biblioteca Laurenziana; 14, Prof. Kurt Weitzmann; 16, Trustees, British Museum; 18-19, Darmstadt, Hessisches Landesmuseum; 21, 22, 31, 34, 35, 39, Paris, Bibliothèque Nationale; 25, Edinburgh, University Library; 26, 32, 33, Prof. Kemal Çig, Istanbul, Topkapi Sarayi Müzesi; 28, 29, 30, Oxford, Clarendon Press; 36, Washington, Smithsonian Institution, Freer Gallery of Art.

PREFACE

No ancient Temple has stimulated as many attempts at archaeological reconstruction or been the object of such repeated imitation and profound theological interpretation in Judaism, Christianity and Islam as the Temple of Solomon.

Only two terse chapters in the Hebrew Bible, I Kings 6-7, are devoted to it. Yet hundreds of books in many languages—Greek, Latin, Arabic, Persian, Hebrew, Aramaic, Syriac, German, French, English, Italian, Dutch, and Spanish—contain lengthy mystical, legendary, typological, philological and archaeological explanations of the significance of the meager biblical account.

The site of Solomon's Temple is sacred to three religions. To Judaism, it represents the glory and splendor of the Golden Age of Solomon in the tenth century B.C.; it was the location of two successive temples, one destroyed by the Babylonians in 586 B.C., the other destroyed by the Romans in 70 A.D. In addition, it is bound up with the hope of a restored temple in the messianic future.

For Christianity, the site of the Temple is intimately linked with the life of Christ recorded in the New Testament; it is a hallowed pilgrimage place that inspired the Crusaders in their zealous mission to reconquer the Holy Land.

To Muslims the site of the ancient Temple is sacred, too, for upon it stands the oldest extant Islamic building, the seventh-century Dome of the Rock, enshrining the legendary stone upon which, according to Muslim tradition, Abraham intended to sacrifice Ishmael, and from which Muhammad ascended to heaven.

Synagogues and churches sometimes consciously strove to embody architectural details of Solomon's Temple in their religious structures and to imitate the ritual appurtenances which had stood within it. The church in the Middle Ages is sometimes referred to as the "New Solomonic Temple"; the synagogue is frequently called "a minor sanctuary" (*mikdash me'at*)—a surrogate for the future messianic Temple.

Kings and emperors—Justinian I in Byzantine Constantinople, Charlemagne in Aachen, Germany, Philip II in Spain, James I in England, Frederick II in Prussia—likened their building projects to Solomon's Temple and strove to surpass it. Their compatriots acclaimed them as new Solomons.

The papers of the five scholars, read at the annual meeting of the Society of Biblical Literature held in Chicago on November 9, 1973, are devoted to some little-known or highly controversial aspects of the Temple of Solomon in the hope of shedding new light on this fascinating subject as well as encouraging further investigation.

J.G.

THE BASIC STRUCTURE OF SOLOMON'S TEMPLE AND ARCHAEOLOGICAL RESEARCH

Jean Ouellette

No exact record exists of the numerous attempts that have been made in the past to reconstruct the Temple of Solomon. Many of these attempts share two common characteristics—the selectivity they employ with respect to the value placed on the ancient sources which happen to preserve a description of the Temple and the intrinsic merit attributed to each one of these sources.[1] Most scholars find it natural to base the essential features of their reconstruction on the description contained in the Hebrew text of I Kings 6-7.[2] However, the extreme terseness of that source forces scholars into adopting a more eclectic approach towards other biblical accounts which can supply additional details essential to any reconstruction of the Temple. Hence it is not uncommon to find in such reconstructions elements that are missing in I Kings 6-7 but have been conveniently borrowed from the parallel account preserved in the Books of Chronicles or, even, from various passages scattered throughout the entire Hebrew Bible. Thus the description of Ezekiel's Temple constitutes for many scholars a major source of information which they can readily tap.[3]

Serious objections can be raised against the eclectic approach, especially if the ultimate intention is an accurate reconstruction of the Temple built by Solomon in the tenth century B.C., before the building underwent any major modifications at the hands of later kings.[4] I do not mean to imply that scholars could produce a more exact reconstruction of the Temple by relying exclusively on the account preserved in the Hebrew text of I Kings 6-7. Scholars are still much too divided as to the inner historical value of the various sections that make up what appears to be the most ancient description of the Temple.

There are scholars who, although aware of the possibility that many editorial additions may have been incorporated into our text at a later date, believe that the account of I Kings 6-7 goes back ultimately to the period when the Temple was being erected. Edouard Dhorme, for example, insists on the archival character of our main source: "A côté des archives du palais, de caractère plutôt profane, il existe des archives du Temple, utilisées par exemple dans I Rois VI-VIII, 13 . . ."[5] Similarly, Martin Noth ascribes to the Temple account a high degree of historical reliability.[6] In spite of many editorial accretions still visible in the text, Noth believes that our document is nonetheless contemporary with the building period of the Temple in its early stage.[7]

Other scholars, however, are more sceptical about the original character of the account preserved in the first Book of Kings and will not attribute to each of its component parts the same degree of historical accuracy. Thus Konrad Rupprecht, relying mainly on Noth's analysis of I Kings 6-7, concludes that the three storied structure described in I Kings 6:5-10 could not have been part of the original building, but must have been added at a subsequent stage of the history of the Temple.[8] Consequently any model of the Temple built according to the specifications of I Kings 6-7, taken at face value, would necessarily include features that came to be incorporated into Solomon's Temple only in the course of time. For Rupprecht, as a matter of fact, there is little in I Kings 6 that directly applies to the original Solomonic Temple.[9]

It becomes obvious that the interpretation of archaeological evidence, relating to the Temple, will often vary with each scholar's treatment of the basic literary sources. Those scholars who are mainly concerned with the study of traditions (*Überlieferungsgeschichte*) and with the editorial history (*Redaktionsgeschichte*) of I Kings 6-7 find little opportunity to discuss the relevant archaeological evidence. On the other hand, by way of contrast, a scholar like Theodor Busink, who strongly emphasizes the importance of archaeological evidence for the study of the Temple, fails to offer a really penetrating exegesis of the ancient sources which he utilizes.[10]

We do not wish to discuss here the proper or the improper use that can be made of archaeological discoveries by biblical scholars anxious to elucidate problems arising from the study of ancient texts. De Vaux's dictum, raised to an axiomatic status by G. Ernest Wright, applies fully in the case of the Temple: "Archaeology does not confirm the text, which is what it is, it can only confirm the interpretation which we give it".[11] In their efforts to find archaeological data relevant to the study of the Temple, scholars are often led to draw hasty parallels with various structures described by archaeologists as Canaanite or Israelite sanctuaries. The most frequently quoted parallels include the temple at Tell Tainat in Syria, the temple of Stratum Ib (LB II) at Hazor and the Iron Age temple at Arad.[12] In each case, scholars justify the comparison by stressing the so-called tripartite division of the Solomonic Temple, a feature which seems to have characterized so many of the temples that have been unearthed in Palestine and Syria.[13]

Even a superficial look at the ground plans of the three temples just mentioned should reveal how basically different they must have been from Solomon's Temple. For the description of I Kings 6:1ff. makes it abundantly clear that Solomon's Temple, which was, in this respect, very similar to the temple at Tell Tainat, conformed to the "long house" type of building. Its plan was, therefore, rectangular and included, at least in the present state of our main source, a vestibule of the "broad room" type, a nave of the "long room" type with an axial entrance situated in one of its short sides and, finally, an adyton described as a perfectly square room.[14]

In spite of obvious differences (for example, the adyton at Tell Tainat, unlike the Solomonic *devir*, is not square), it would seem to us that the general plan of the Tell Tainat temple resembles the ground plan of Solomon's Temple more than any other sanctuary excavated in recent years (fig. 1).[15] Busink has insisted too much, in our opinion, in stressing the differences that exist between the two sanctuaries and his analysis has exceeded the limits imposed by the description of I Kings 6-7.[16] There is certainly no justification in the Hebrew text for Busink's contention that the entrance to the Solomonic *ulam* had side-panels ("Seitenflächen"), a feature that would stand in sharp contrast, according to him, with the Tell Tainat temple where the entrance of the vestibule occupies the full width of the building.[17] Moreover, Busink's contention that the *devir*, unlike the adyton at Tell Tainat, was architecturally distinct from the *hekhal* is baseless.[18] Quite to the contrary, one can show on the basis of I Kings 6:16ff. that the *devir* was obtained by partitioning, from the inside, the main room of the Temple.[19]

With regard to the Iron Age temple excavated at Tell Arad (fig. 2) by Yohanan Aharoni, much has been written in recent years about its possible relationship to the Solomonic Temple.[20] According to Aharoni himself, the plan of the sanctuary in Arad is "the essential plan of the Jerusalem temple".[21] We would agree with Yigael Yadin that this claim is unwarranted, although similarities of another kind cannot be denied, such as, for example, the presence of an altar in the courtyards of both temples.[22] But the differences in the ground plans of the two temples are equally striking. First, the temple at Arad had no built-up porch. This is, of course, in sharp contrast to the description of I Kings 6:3ff., at least in its present state. We might concede to Aharoni that the Solomonic Temple could have been for some time without an *ulam* in view of the fact that the measurements of the House in I Kings 6:2 do not include the vestibule.[23]

A second major difference can be seen in the basic plans of the two main rooms. In Jerusalem, the *hekhal* conformed to the long room type of construction while at Arad the corresponding room was a distinct broad room.[24] Finally, the Holy of Holies is represented at Arad only by a niche whereas in Jerusalem the *devir*, although obtained by the mere partitioning of the *hekhal* (see above n.19), had all the appearances of a separate room.

We must now turn to the evidence available at Hazor. In the temple found in Stratum Ib (fourteenth cent. B.C.), Yadin has urged scholars to see a "prototype" of Solomon's Temple.[25] The basic plan of the Hazor temple (fig. 3) comprises "three elements following each other with the doorways on a single axis leading to each chamber in succession".[26] But there ends, in our opinion, the similarity with the temple described in I Kings 6-7. The entrance hall (2128) measured 9.8 x 4.8m and may be compared with the Solomonic *ulam* only insofar as both porches were of the broadroom type. At Hazor, however, the porch was narrower than the front of the temple while in Jerusalem the *ulam* occupied the full width of the *hekhal*.[27] As to the middle hall (2129), it was almost square (5.8 x 5m) and thus can hardly be compared with the *hekhal* which was much longer than wide (40 x 20 cubits).[28] There was also a rear hall

(2123), the biggest in size (13.3 x 8m) since, according to Yadin, it occupied roughly the previous temple's main hall.[29] The niche (2116) carved in the center of the back wall further accentuates the differences that exist between this sanctuary and the Solomonic Temple.[30]

We cannot review here at length the incredible amount of literature dealing with the pillars Jakhin and Boaz, certainly the most controversial feature of Solomon's Temple.[31] As is well known, the two pillars are believed by a majority of scholars to have had a purely decorative and symbolic function.[32]

Only a few scholars would ascribe to Jakhin and Boaz, over and above their symbolic significance, a practical function. Robertson Smith, for example, suggested long ago that the two pillars were built "on the model of those candlesticks which we find represented on Phoenician monuments", a theory that has been revived more recently by William Albright for whom Jakhin and Boaz served as "lofty cressets".[33] For Samuel Yeivin, who draws an analogy with a custom current among the nomadic tribes of pre-Islamic Arabia, the columns Jakhin and Boaz, although free-standing, symbolized in front of the Temple "the permanent abiding of Yahweh."[34]

It seems to us that scholars have been overly preoccupied with the symbolism of the two pillars and have not paid enough attention to some very significant details in the textual tradition available to us. Thus we learn from LXX III Kings 7:9 that an architrave *(mélathron)* rested on top of the two pillars which, in turn, is somewhat vaguely *(katà tò ailàm)* related to the *ulam*.[35] This indication, in itself, may prove fatal to all the theories advocating the freestanding character of Jakhin and Boaz.

We have argued in a previous study dealing with the problems relating to the Solomonic *ulam*, mainly on the basis of I Kings 6:4, that the vestibule of Solomon's Temple conformed to the *bît ḥilâni* type of portico.[36] If this were the case, the pillars Jakhin and Boaz could indeed have been part of the structure itself as supports either for the roof or even perhaps for a sort of awning or canopy that might have projected in front of the vestibule and which is conveniently illustrated on the pottery model of a small chapel from Idalion in Cyprus (fig. 4).[37] It is interesting to note, in this connection, that such a feature, known in Hebrew as *'b*, seems to have been appended to an *ulam* that is not otherwise clearly identified in I Kings 7:6 (see also Ezek. 41:25).[38]

Contrary to Rupprecht's statement, our reading of I Kings 6:4 does not involve any textual change.[39] We simply proposed to read the two words *lbyt ḥlwny* as one expression defining the *ḥilâni* character of the Solomonic vestibule. As for the words *šqphym* and *'ṭmym*, we would like to suggest that the former may perhaps be a gloss on the rare and obscure *'ṭmym*, which we derive from the Dravidian languages with the meaning 'towers'.[40] As a matter of fact, we know that *bît ḥilânis* often had a tower at one of their corners (fig. 5).[41]

With regard to free-standing pillars, we think that these must have been quite rare in the Ancient Orient so that scholars should be extremely cautious in drawing analogies with Jakhin and Boaz.[42] Possibly the clearest example of free-standing pillars comes from Kouyunjik on a relief drawn by Layard and representing, according to Richard Barnett, the flight of King Luli of Sidon from the city of Tyre, as recorded in the annals of Sennacherib.[43] On this relief, one can distinguish a building, "its arched entrance flanked by two great free standing columns with fleur-de-lys capitals" (fig. 6). For Barnett, these two pillars can be identified with the twin columns of pure gold and emerald (or malachite) described by Herodotus (II, 44) as belonging to the temple of Herakles-Melkart at Tyre and he proposes to consider them as the "prototypes of the biblical Jakhin and Boaz".[44]

But is it so certain that the pillars on Layard's relief were completely free standing? While the drawing published by Barnett makes it abundantly clear that the columns did not support the roof of the building in question, the possibility remains that they might have been topped by an awning similar to the one featured on the clay model temple from Idalion which Barnett himself cites as a parallel.[45] And the fact that the relief is blurred near the top of the pillars might very well be an indication that something is missing on Layard's drawing.

The site of biblical Arad has also provided archaeological parallels to Jakhin and Boaz. There two stone bases were found flanking the entrance to the *hekhal*, in that part of the courtyard which served in lieu of an *ulam* since, as we have seen, the sanctuary was without a built up porch.[46] Arguing from II Chron. 3:17 which states that Solomon set up the two pillars "in front of the Holy Place" (*'l pny hhykl*) Aharoni has attempted to show that in Jerusalem too the pillars Jakhin and Boaz could have stood "in the *ulam* at the entrance to the *hekhal*" and not in the court, therefore suggesting that the Solomonic *ulam* was an open porch.[47] We find no basic objection to this view. One should, however, not argue here on the strength of II Chron. 3:17 since the term *hykl* used in this passage designates, as in many other instances, the Temple as a whole and not necessarily its middle room. Jakhin and Boaz, then, can certainly be visualized "in front of the House" (*lpny hbyt*), as stated explicitly in II Chron. 3:15.[48]

It is equally difficult to ascertain the exact relationship of Jakhin and Boaz to the *ulam*. Two rather obscure verses (I Kings 7:19 and 21) seem to indicate that the twin pillars did in fact belong to the vestibule of the Temple. Even if we were to discard the expression *b'wlm* in I Kings 7:19 as secondary, following what seems to be the majority opinion, there would remain the explicit statement of I Kings 7:21: "He set up the pillars of the vestibule (*lwlm*) of the Temple."[49] The comparison with the temple at Tell Tainat can prove once more useful at this point.

There the two columns were situated well within the first room of the sanctuary. And yet Henri Frankfort has thought it proper to describe this building as a temple with columns "in antis".[50] The position of these two columns does not differ greatly from the position of the three pillars that stood in the porch of the adjacent ḫilâni-palace. We see no compelling reason for imagining a much different position for Jakhin and Boaz. One might prefer, however, the arrangement that prevailed at Hazor in the temple of Stratum I A (LB III).[51] There, according to Yadin, conical pillar bases were found inside the porch, in front of the threshold (2101) separating the vestibule (2118) from the main hall (2115). We are told by the excavator himself that the two pillars had no "structural" function. If this were indeed the case, we would have here a very cogent argument in favor of the free standing character of Jakhin and Boaz.[52]

The only other possibility would be to suppose, with Busink, that I Kings 7:19 refers to another set of columns entirely different from Jakhin and Boaz so that any archaeological model of the Temple would have to show at least four columns on the façade. The pair composed of Jakhin and Boaz would have stood as a free standing ornament in front of the building while another pair would have stood in the entrance and would have been part of the entire structure.[53]

1. For a convenient survey of these sources, see Th. A. Busink, *Der Tempel von Jerusalem* (Leiden, 1970), 22-44.
2. See Busink, *op cit.*, 44ff. for a review of the best reconstructions of the Temple that are on record.
3. A good example of this procedure is the common and very reasonable assumption that there was a flight of steps leading to the Vestibule. Scholars argue here on the strength of Ezek. 41:8 which states that the Temple was built on a raised platform (*gbh*) six cubits high. As to the steps, they are explicitly mentioned in Ezek. 40:49. In the Septuagintal transmission of this verse, we are told that there were ten steps leading up to the *ulam*. This idea of a raised platform underneath the Temple has engendered much speculation. For the most recent discussion, see Busink, *op. cit.*, 171. Cf. also L. Waterman, "The Damaged 'Blueprints' of the Temple of Solomon", *JNES* 2 (1943), 284-294, 385; P.L. Garber, "Resurrecting Solomon's Temple", *BA* 14 (1951), 2-24, 7; A. Parrot, *Le Temple de Jérusalem* (Paris, 1954), 16; G.E. Wright, *Biblical Archaeology* (London, 1962), 138, 140; L.H. Vincent and A.M. Steve, *Jérusalem de l'Ancien Testament* (Paris, 1956), 481. Another controversial feature is the crenelated parapet that crowns many representations of the Temple. Scholars argue in this case from Deut. 22:8 where a *m'qh* is said to have been required for all buildings. On this, see G.E. Wright, "The Steven's Reconstruction of the Solomonic Temple," *BA* 18 (1955), 43-44, 42, fig. 9.
4. See for example the innovations undertaken by King Josiah in II Kings 22:4ff.
5. Cf. *La Bible* I (Paris, 1956), LXXXIV.
6. See his *Könige*, I, BK IX/1 (Neukirchen, 1968), 95-129. As

pointed out by K. Rupprecht in "Nachrichtungen von Erweiterung und Renovierung des Tempels in 1 Könige 6", *ZDPV* 88(1972), 38-52, 39, Noth's views on the Temple differ from the conceptions of earlier critics mainly by their methodological intent. He assumes for I King 6 a "*Überlieferungskette*" (see Rupprecht, art. cit., 39) that takes us directly back into the period of the royal building activity in Jerusalem: cf. Noth, *op. cit.,* 106. The conclusions reached by Noth have been accepted, for the most part, by J. Gray in *I and II Kings* (Philadelphia, 1963), 157ff.

7. On the secondary character of several verses as analyzed by Noth, cf. Rupprecht, art. cit., 39.

8. "Dieses Verständnis von v.7 setzt notwendig voraus, dass der dreigeschossige Anbau rings um Hekal und Debir erst in einem späteren Stadium nach der Tempelweihe aufgeführt wurde": Rupprecht, art. cit., 47. On the side-structure of the Temple, see our study, "The Yâṣîaʻ and the Ṣelâʻôt: Two Mysterious Structures in Solomon's Temple", *JNES* 31 (1972), 187-191.

9. "Wir meinen jedoch, in 1 R.6 einen derartigen Reflex späterer Baugeschichte sehen zu sollen, und zwar innerhalb des ersten grösseren Abschnitts dieses Kapitels: innerhalb der Verse 1-10": Rupprecht, art. cit., 39.

10. See the remarks to that effect of G. Krautwurst in his review of Busink's monumental work *Der Tempel von Jerusalem* (cf. above n. 1) in *ZDPV* 88(1972),91: ". . . bietet der Verf. zwar keine eingehende exegetische Analyse der betreffenden Texte . . ."

11. See R. de Vaux, "On Right and Wrong Uses of Archaeology", in *Near Eastern Archaeology in the Twentieth Century*, ed. J.

A. Sanders (New York, 1970), 64-80, 78 and G.E. Wright, "What Archaeology Can and Cannot Do", *BA* 34 (1971), 70-76, 76.

12. On Tell Tainat, cf. C.W. McEwan, "The Syrian Expedition of the Oriental Institute of the University of Chicago", *AJA* 41(1937), 8-13, esp. 9, fig. 4. The final report is available in R.C. Haines, *Excavations in the Plain of Antioch,* vol. 2, O.I.P. 95(Chicago, 1971): see review by R.S. Ellis in *JNES* 32(1973), 256-258. On the Hazor temple, see now Y. Yadin, *Hazor* (London, 1972), 83-87. On the Arad temple, cf. Y. Aharoni, "The Negev", in *Archaeology and Old Testament Study*, ed. D. Winton Thomas (Oxford, 1967), 385-403, 395-397; id., "Arad: Its Inscriptions and Temple", *BA* 31(1968), 2-32, esp. 18ff.; id., "Israelite Temples in the Period of the Monarchy", *Proceedings of the Fifth World Congress of Jewish Studies* I (Jerusalem, 1971), 69-74. For a review of the new archaeological evidence pertaining to the site of Solomon's Temple, see K. Kenyon. "New Evidence on Solomon's Temple", *MUSJ* 46(1970), 139-149.

13. For a most recent attempt to describe a newly excavated temple in terms of the Solomonic sanctuary, see A. Mazar, "A Philistine Temple at Tell Qasile", *BA* 36(1973), 42-48, 45. Another temple often cited in connection with the Solomonic Temple is the Baal sanctuary at Ugarit: cf. Busink, *op. cit.,* 478ff. J. Gray sees in the Baal and in the Dagon temples at Ugarit the earliest examples of "the tripartite temple of outer court with the great altar, inner court or hall, and inmost shrine;" cf. *"ḥâṣêr, hêkâl,* and *debîr* of Solomon's temple:" see "Ugarit" in *Archaeology and Old Testament Study,* ed. D. Winton Thomas, etc., 145-167, 147.

14. Scholars often overlook the fact that II Chron. 3:4 hesitates as

to the exact position of the *ulam* vis-à-vis the *hekhal*. According to I Kings 6:3, the main axis of the *hekhal* was perpendicular, and not parallel, to the long side of the vestibule. But the Chronicler has preserved a text that could lend some support for just the opposite arrangement since it juxtaposes to *'lpny rḥb hbyt* of I Kings 6:3 the phrase *'l pny h'rk*. For a convenient display of temples with a plan conforming to the long room type, see O. Keel, *Die Welt der altorientalischen Bildsymbolik und das Alte Testament* (Zurich, 1972), 133.

15. A. Kuschke regards the Tell Tainat temple as the "nachsliegende altorientalische Parallele" to the Solomonic Temple": cf. *Das Ferne und Nahe Wort* (Festschrift Leonard Rose) (Berlin, 1967), "Der Tempel Salomos und der syrische Tempeltypus", 124-132, 132. See also W.F. Albright, "The Old Testament and the Archaeology of the Ancient East" in *The Old Testament and Modern Study,* ed. H.H. Rowley (London, 1951), 27-47, 36 and A.G. Barrois, *Manuel d'archéologie biblique* II (Paris, 1953), 443.

16. See *Der Tempel von Jerusalem,* 561-562.

17. *Ibid.*, 561.

18. "Das Debir des salomonischen Tempels war ein im hinteren Teil der Zella errichteter geschlossener Holzbau von quadratischem Grundriss; in *tell tainat* bildet das Allerheiligste einen einheitlichen Teil des Gebäudes und eine räumliche Einheit mit der Zella": *ibid.*, 561.

19. This conclusion rests mainly on the analysis of *yrkty* in I Kings 6:16. See our study, "The Solomonic Debir according to the Hebrew Text of I Kings 6", *JBL* 89(1970), 338-343. It is interesting to note that Busink had defended earlier the view

that the Holy of Holies was a sort of *"naiskos"* built within the cella: cf. "Les origines du Temple de Salomon", *JEOL* 17(1963), 165-192, 186. For a comparative study of the Hebrew and Greek versions bearing on these problems, see D.W. Gooding, "Temple Specifications in MT and LXX", *VT* 17(1967), 143-172.

20. See above n. 12.
21. Cf. art. cit., in *Archaeology and Old Testament Study*, 395.
22. On some of the differences between the Arad temple and the Temple in Jerusalem, see Yadin, *Hazor*, 86, n.4.
23. Cf. Aharoni, art. cit., *BA* 31(1968), 22. Aharoni rightly points out that the *ulam* was built in a special sort of masonry similar to that of the court (cf. I Kings 7:12). On this technique and its use in ancient architecture, notably at Tell Tainat, see our study "Le vestibule du Temple de Salomon était-il un bît ḥilâni", *RB* 76(1969), 365-378, 378, esp. nn. 74-75.
24. Cf. Aharoni, *ibid.*, 19 and 25. The origin of the long room is still much in dispute. K. Möhlenbrink, *Der Tempel Salomos* (Stuttgart, 1932), derived the long cella of Solomon's Temple from the Assyrian long room: see p. 102. For a recent discussion of this opinion, cf. Busink, *Der Tempel von Jerusalem,* 576ff. One must not confuse the long room type of construction, characterized by an axial entrance in one of the short sides, with the type of building featuring what H. Frankfort has called a "bent-axis" approach: see *The Art and Architecture of the Ancient Orient* (Baltimore, 1963), 21, 23ff. For a comparative study of these two types of temples in Mesopotamia, see A. Spycket, *Les statues de culte dans les textes mésopotamiens des origines à la Ire dynastie de Babylone* (Paris, 1968), 9-10.
25. See Y. Yadin, "Excavations at Hazor", in *The Biblical Archaeologist Reader,* 2, ed. D.N. Freedman and E.F.

Campbell, Jr. (New York, 1964), 191-247, 218; "Hazor", *Archaeology and Old Testament Study*, etc., 245-263, 251; Hazor, etc., 83ff. and 88, fig. 20.

26. Yadin, *Hazor*, 86 and Businck, *Der Tempel von Jerusalem*, 398, fig. 100.

27. Compare I Kings 6:3 with Yadin's description of the situation at Hazor: *op. cit.*, 85.

28. Cf. I Kings 6:2.

29. See Yadin, *op. cit.*, 83.

30. *Ibid.*, 84.

31. For a convenient survey of scholarly opinion, see Businck, *op. cit.*, 312ff. See also our study, *RB* 76(1969), 375-378. The standard opinion is well represented by B.D. Eerdman's statement concerning the two pillars: "Yet there is no evidence that they had in Jerusalem any other meaning than of stylish ornaments". Cf. *The Religion of Israel* (Leiden, 1947), 64.

32. For a detailed treatment of the whole question, see A. Audin, "Les piliers jumeaux", *Archiv Orientální* 21(1953), 430-439; *id.*, "Les piliers jumeaux dans le monde sémitique," *Archiv Orientální* 21 (1953), 430-439; W. Kornfeld, "Der Symbolismus der Tempelsäule", *ZAW* 74(1962), 50-57.

33. See Robertson Smith, *The Religion of the Semites* (1 ed. 1889), New York, 1972, p. 488 and W.F. Albright, "Two Cressets from Marissa and the Pillars of Jakhin and Boaz", *BASOR* 85(1942), 18-27. See also our criticism of Albright's theory in our study, *RB* 76(1969), 377. It is interesting to note that Robertson Smith had difficulty with his own views on the pillars: "It seems difficult to believe that the enormous pillars . . . were actually used as fire-altars: but if they were, the presumption is that the cressets were fed with the suet of the sacrifice". Cf. *op. cit.*, 488.

34. Cf. S. Yeivin, "Jachin and Boaz", *PEQ* 91(1959), 6-22, 20-21. See also, by the same author, "Jakhin and Boaz" (in Hebrew), *EI* 5(1958), 97-104, 103-104.

35. See our study, *RB* 76(1969), 376ff.

36. *Ibid.*, 365ff.

37. Möhlenbrink, in *Der Tempel Salomos*, 111, envisages the first alternative. Yeivin thinks that the two columns of the pottery model from Idalion were not originally connected with the structure: cf. art. cit., *PDQ* 91 (1959), 10 and pl. 1, fig. 1. See also O. Keel, *Die Welt der altorientalischen Bildsymbolik und das Alte Testament*, 144 and 145, fig. 125.

38. Gray connects Hebrew *'b* with Arabic *'abba*, 'to be superabundant' in I and II Kings, 168-169. For H. Weidhaas, who compares the *'b* of I Kings 7:6 to a canopy (Akk. *ṣululu*) erected by King Sennacherib and suggests that these terms may designate the platforms used for the royal audiences ("*Audienzbaldachin*"): cf. "*Der bit ḫilani*," *ZA* 45(1939), 108-168, 115, n. 2 and 118-119. See also M. Rutten, *Les arts du Moyen-Orient Ancien* (Paris, 1962), 136.

39. Cf. Rupprecht's remarks in "Nachrichten von Erweiterung und Renovierung des Tempels in I Könige 6," *ZDPV* 88(1972), 40, n. 21.

40. Thus the expression *'ṭmht' dšwr'* in *Eruvin*, 57b would mean "the turrets of the wall." We have gathered the evidence for such an understanding of *'ṭmym* in a study entitled "The Dravidian Origin of Hebrew *'ṭmym* in I Kings 6:4," in the *Bulletin of the Institute of Jewish Studies* 2(1974), 99-102.

41. See our study mentioned in n. 40 and also Yadin's remark in *BA* 23(1970), 74.

42. The earliest free-standing pillars known in Mesopotamia belonged to the Pillars Temple of the Eanna precinct at

Warka, level Ib: cf. A. L. Perkins, *The Comparative Archaeology of Early Mesopotamia* (Chicago, 1963), 122. But see also the claim made by G. Contenau in favor of free-standing pillars found at Tell-Obeid in *Manuel d'archéologie orientale* I (Paris, 1927), 464; 438, fig. 334.

43. See R. D. Barnett, "Ezekiel and Tyre", *EI* 9(1969), 6-13, and pl. I.

44. See *ibid.*, 7. Practically all studies on Jakhin and Boaz mention Herodotus' testimony: cf. R. de Vaux, *Les Institutions de l'Ancien Testament* II (Paris, 1960), 150. There is also a statement by Strabo (III, 5, 5) who refers to two copper pillars (8 cubits high) erected in the Phoenician colony of Gades in Spain in honor of Hercules. On this, see A. Audin, "Les piliers jumeaux dans le monde sémitique", *Archiv Orientální* 21(1953), 438. Cf. also D. Harden, *The Phoenicians* (New York, 1963), 86; 224, n. 59. Another literary document comes from Lucian (16-28) who mentions the presence of two pillars (55 m. high!) in front of the temple of Atargatis at Heliopolis: see de Vaux, *op. cit.*, II, 150.

45. Barnett, art. cit., 7. See also above n. 37.

46. Cf. Aharoni, art. cit., *BA* 31(1968), 22 and fig. 15, 23.

47. Aharoni, *ibid.*, 22.

48. On this point, see our remarks in art. cit., *RB* 76(1969), 375, esp. 58.

49. On *b'wlm* and *l'lm*, see our study, *RB* 76(1969), 366, n. 3 and 375. See also Busink, *Der Tempel von Jerusalem*, 175, n. 39.

50. See *The Art and Architecture of the Ancient Orient*, 175; cf. also our remarks in *RB* 76(1969), 375, n. 61 and 376, fig. 4.

51. Cf. Yadin, *Hazor*, 88, fig. 21.

52. Yadin himself, of course, stresses the relevance of his

discovery for the proper understanding of Jakhin and Boaz: *ibid.*, 89.

53. See above n. 49. Cf. also Busink, *op. cit.*, Abb. 52.

THE TEMPLE OF SOLOMON IN EARLY CHRISTIAN AND BYZANTINE ART

Stanley Ferber

It is hard to imagine that the great Temple built by Solomon in Jerusalem, and so completely described in Kings and Chronicles, should not have made an impact upon the art of the Early Christians. Yet during the first seven centuries of the Christian Era the Temple Precinct, in all likelihood, was a barren platform, devoid of any architectural survival of the imposing structure built by Solomon.[1] What, in lieu of the actual structure, inspired the Early Christian artist? What formulae or conceits were used to conjure up the vision of the Temple to his audience?

In attempting to arrive at an answer to these questions it will be necessary to deal with a variety of disparate objects. They will vary as to style, genre, date and provenance. But all are related by virtue of their vision of our theme: the Temple of Solomon. In examining and discussing these various objects our attempt will be to separate the constant elements from the variable ones, and by relating the specific images to either analogous material or historical setting, ultimately arrive at archetypes for the images in question.

The visual material and problems with which I will deal should be distinguished from what is essentially a non-visual, metaphoric approach to Solomon's Temple.[2] This approach is best exemplified by Eusebius of Caesarea's characterization of Paulinus, the early fourth-century Bishop of Tyre, famous as a builder and restorer of churches. Eusebius asks, rhetorically: "Whether one should call thee a new Bezalel, the architect of a divine tabernacle, or Solomon, the king of a new and far goodlier Jerusalem, or even a new Zerubbabel, who bestowed upon the temple of God that glory which greatly exceeded the former?"[3] Eusebius continues his panegyric, declaring that Paulinus "... in no wise doth come behind that Bezalel, whom God himself filled with the spirit of wisdom and understanding and with the knowledge as well of crafts and sciences, and called him to be the workman that should construct the temple of heavenly types in symbolic fashion."[4] But just what did the temple of "this new and goodly Zerubbabel" look like? The description which Eusebius gives of Paulinus' new structure, when one tries to separate the hyperbole and images from tangible, architectural reality, is that of a fourth-century basilica, possibly preceded by a narthex and an atrium within which was a fountain. It appeared, in all probability, like the fifth-century church of St. John of the Studion in Constantinople. As such there is no apparent relationship to the ancient Near Eastern Temple type that most scholars now accept as the type of Solomon's Temple.[5] Indeed, there is no reason to expect the Early Christians to have had this type of historical or archaeological awareness. However, in describing the richness and elaborateness of the decoration of Paulinus' "temple", Eusebius describes it with phrases from Psalms which refer to the cedars of Lebanon used as roofing beams, just as Solomon roofed the Temple with boards of cedar. Thus in referring to the builder of the new Christian church and its appurtenances, Eusebius writes, "These also were wrought by our most peaceful Solomon, who built the temple of God . . ."[6]

This approach to the Temple of Solomon as a prefiguration of the Temple of God, the Church of the New Law established by Christ, is suggested elsewhere in Eusebius and more directly in its fullest allegorical sense by Prudentius in his *Lines to be Inscribed Under Scenes from History* written *ca.* 400: "Wisdom builds a temple by Solomon's hands . . ."[7] To the best of my knowledge no Early Christian representation has been preserved which illustrates this particular verse of Prudentius, although it has been suggested that all 48 quatrains of the poem were intended as instructions for artists or as inscriptions for an already existing series of New Testament scenes and Old Testament antetypes.[8] The only depiction I know of which may be considered somewhat analogous to the verse and which most probably had a fifth-century source can be found in a tenth-century copy of Prudentius' *Psychomachia*. In this work we see a personification of Wisdom seated in the Temple of Wisdom.[9] Beyond this possible reflection of an earlier source I know of no illustration from the Early Christian era which displays the visual vocabulary to illustrate the allegorical language of this particular theme of Christian exegesis. The artist had to work within the framework of known forms so that they would be recognized by his audience, while at the same time imbuing them with a contextual meaning that separated them from their non-Christian sources. I would suggest that the absence of any Early Christian allegorical representations of the Temple is largely due to this problem.[10]

A second approach to the Temple is one which finds actual manifestation in illustrations. Two examples of this approach fall within our Early Christian domain: one is an illustration in the Codex Amiatinus, to which we will return later, and the other, the earliest extant narrative/descriptive illustration of the Temple known to me.

This latter example is found in a fragmentary Old Testament manuscript known as the Quedlinburg Itala.[11] Of what had probably been an illuminated Book of Kings, only five leaves have been preserved; portions of Samuel and Kings. Textual and paleographic evidence suggest that the leaves can be dated as early as the late fourth or early fifth century. Fortunately, for our purposes, two of the passages from I Kings contain illustrations: one illustrating the embassy of Solomon to Hiram, and the other, the Feast of the Dedication of the Temple. The latter illustration is in an extremely poor state of preservation, but is especially revealing because of its deterioration. This seeming paradox is explained by the revelation of a text under the flaking paint which gives careful instructions to the miniaturist as to just what he was to depict. It reads as follows:

Make a tripartite scene. Make King Solomon where he sent a message to King Hiram asking him to send carpenters to help with the building of the Temple. Make the workshop where the workmen of King Solomon and King Hiram build the Golden House and bronze columns and between and above them make two rows of pomegranates and make a molten sea and make twelve bronze fruits on the four corners of the ceiling . . . and within the temple the bronze lions and crowns and the cherubim and the braided borders . . . make also the place where Solomon will sacrifice before the Lord and kneeling with extended arms will pray and where all the people with him stood praying before the Lord.[12]

The remains of the illustration so carefully mandated obviously do not follow the directions. The artist, for whatever reason, has chosen to follow another tradition—one rather interesting for us. His depiction of the Temple follows what appears to be a Late Antique convention for cities and temples. Examples, such as the scene from the Milan Iliad (fig. 7) of the mid-fifth century show a similar configuration of city-walls and buildings, as do the city conventions for Jerusalem and Bethlehem (fig. 8) found in the mosaic on the triumphal arch of the fifth-century church of S. Maria Maggiore in Rome. Only the still visible inscriptions *Templum* above the city-walls and *Salomon orans* above a kneeling figure outside the city-walls, relate the Itala illustration to the specific instructions given to the painter. On the other hand, there is a rather strange, anomalous illustration in the Bible of San Pedro de Roda of the eleventh century.[13] This Spanish manuscript provides us with an area of interesting speculation related to the text instructions for the Itala artist. If we examine the illustration in question, on fol. 129v (fig. 9), and usually called "The History of Solomon and Building the Temple", we find a scene which is roughly tripartite: a vertical rectangular part to the left depicting, in the upper register, Solomon sending a messenger to Hiram; messenger in route in the middle register, and Hiram dispatching his men in the lowest register. The second of the tripartite scenes is roughly square, and to the right of the rectangular section. The lowest register in this portion contains a depiction which apparently has no bearing upon our topic for it may be a scene of the Queen of Sheba coming to Solomon. But the register immediately above shows an altar with two sacrificial animals on it, and a figure (Solomon) in a strange, kneeling, arms thrust out position, being blessed by the hand of God. He is attended by three priest-like figures. The third of the tripartite scenes is immediately above and contains a depiction of the Ark of the Covenant flanked by two cherubim. The multiple arcade above contains the busts of twelve people, a reference to the twelve tribes of Israel; that is, in the Itala directions, "when all the people with him stood praying before the Lord." The scene above with city walls, towers and fighting knights may have some reference to the Heavenly Jerusalem, but does not appear to be part of the "History of Solomon and the Temple." If, indeed, this interpretation of the Roda Bible illumination is correct and follows, however broadly, the general instructions of the Itala scene, we are then faced with two very old traditions. Clearly, the Itala depiction is quite different from what the instructions prescribe, and equally different from the Roda example. On the other hand, the Roda example appears related to the Itala instructions. On this limited evidence, we would suggest two independent traditions preceding the illustration of the Quedlinburg Itala: The one, evident in the Quedlinburg manuscript, dependent upon Late Antique architectural and city-scape conventions, and adapted to the needs of Old Testament illustration. The other tradition, which we have illustrated only in the eleventh-century Roda example, is based upon a set of written instructions for the depiction of the scene; instructions which not only predate the Vulgate, but could, I would suggest, even predate the Itala itself, and represent a tradition foreign to the producers of the Quedlinburg manuscript. Just what this was is a matter open to speculation.[14]

To return to the Codex Amiatinus, mentioned earlier. The manuscript, dating from the end of the seventh century,[15] contains an illumination of the earliest *plan* of the Tabernacle known to me (fig. 10). The plan spans two folios, 2v and 3r, of the present foliation. This manuscript, produced in Northumbria at the twin monasteries of Wearmouth-Jarrow is of special interest to us for a number of reasons. Although of a late seventh-century date, it is fairly certain a faithful copy of the *Codex Grandior*,[16] one of the great pandects Cassiodorus had produced at Vivarium in the sixth century. Further, of direct interest to our problem, Cassiodorus himself had referred to this illustration. In his commentaries on Psalm 86 he refers to the Tabernacle and Temple and says: "Indeed, we ourself, have had painted the Tabernacle which was the first image of the Temple itself, and had it placed in the body of our larger pandect: where, what the text of Divine Scripture itself expresses, is rendered more clearly visually."[17]

The image of which Cassiodorus writes, if we follow the illustration in the Codex Amiatinus is ambiguous and incomplete, but at the same time literally accurate. The large columnar rectangle, the perimeter of the "Temple", has cloth-like draperies hung between the columns, suggesting the possibility of a tent. Cassiodorus, in his commentary on Psalm 14 writes: "For even in the Old Testament the Lord commands a Tabernacle to be made for himself while the Israelite people were in camp, so that the divine house was moved at the same time with the dwellings of the Hebrews."[18] Thus, although Cassiodorus speaks of the Tabernacle and Temple in the commentary on Psalm 86, in the Psalm 14 commentary he speaks of the Tabernacle *within* a structure which was movable, a tent, like the dwellings of the Israelites in the desert.

Shown within the perimeter of this columnar rectangle is the plan of a structure which corresponds to the description of the Tabernacle in the desert, starting at Exodus 25.10-22 and repeated in III Kings 7.48-50. This plan is a small rectangle within which two chambers are clearly demarcated. The first of these chambers, entered through a doorway labelled INTROITUS contains depictions of various liturgical items. Among these we can see the golden table for the showbread, labelled MENSA, the great seven branched *menorah*, $\overline{\text{CAND}}$, and the altar for incense, labelled ALTAR $\overline{\text{THYM}}$. Beyond this room is a smaller chamber labelled $\overline{\text{SCA}}$ $\overline{\text{SCORUM}}$. Within this space is a golden, box-like object on short legs, ARCA $\overline{\text{TEST}}$, and upon this box are winged figures, also in gold, the cherubim. In the forecourt of the Temple we find depictions of the altar of burnt offerings, ALTARE HOLOCAUSTI, and a large amphora, LABRUM. Below the altar of burnt offerings are inscriptions of the names of Moses and Aaron.

In the Codex Amiatinus diagram the four cardinal directions are indicated by the Greek words *arctos, dysis, anatol*, and *mesembria*. The initial letters of these four words spell Adam.

The association of Adam with the cardinal points appears in apocryphal literature as early as the Sibylline Oracles. "Yea it is God himself who fashioned four lettered Adam, the first man fashioned, who completes in his name morn and dusk, antarctic and arctic."[19] A later, and equally widespread apocryphal book, to carry this concept further was the *Book of the Secrets of Enoch*: "And I appointed him a name, from the four component parts, from east, from west, from south, from north, . . . and I called him Adam."[20] Both of these works are of Jewish origin, probably of

Egyptian provenance, and date to the pre-Christian era. Although both works were known and circulated throughout the Mediterranean world, I would like to stress their Jewish, Alexandrian origin, and both of roughly the same time period—second to first century B.C.[21]

Thus in interpreting the Tabernacle/Temple plan of the Codex Amiatinus we see an illustration which exhibits elements of Cassiodorus' commentaries on Psalm 14 and Psalm 86—a view which presents us with the Tabernacle in the desert as a prefiguration of the Temple in Jerusalem, combined with an image that is apparently based upon Jewish apocryphal literature. This type of illustrative presentation is justified by Cassiodorus by frequently citing Josephus in both of the commentaries on the Psalms just mentioned.[22]

For the purposes of our speculations, the use of Josephus as an authority has two implications: Jewish sources had particular weight when dealing with specifically Old Testament material, and more important for this paper, Josephus was heir to a specific tradition which Cassiodorus chose to continue in his *Codex Grandior*. Since no early illustrated Josephus manuscripts have been preserved, and there is even question as to whether there were early illustrated Josephus manuscripts,[23] this sweeping statement cannot be substantiated. But I can present some diverse samples of evidence in partial support of this hypothesis.

But first, by now it must be evident that we are no longer dealing with a specific image of Solomon's Temple, but rather with traditions that mix and/or combine elements of the Temple and Tabernacle. Within this framework, the first example I would like to cite is a Pentateuch fragment known as the "First Leningrad Bible" (fig. 11). The manuscript has a colophon which names the scribe, Solomon ha-Levi ben Bouya'a, and date of completion, corresponding to November, 929.[24]

Of specific interest to us is the fragmentary illustration of the Temple/Tabernacle. Under a gable form, filled with a vine rinceaux pattern we see the tablets of the Law within an ark-like shrine. The two leaf-like forms flanking the ark may be intended to represent the cherubim or perhaps some form of the "Tree of Life."[25] Below this unit we see a depiction of the *menorah*, the seven-branched lampstand, which rests upon a triple-arched gateway. Although it is only three-arched, the unit is made up of five segments, perhaps corresponding to the five openings of the Tent of the Tabernacle as indicated in Exodus 26.37. Flanking the ark and *menorah* are schematic representations of the various liturgical utensils associated with Temple ritual. The identification of the specific objects need not concern us here.

In the same tradition, formally related by its schematic, diagrammatic, non-illusionistic treatment of the same theme, is a copper and bronze Torah case of Samaritan origin (fig. 12). Dating from the seventeenth century, it is reputedly a copy of an older, silver case taken from the Samaritans by the Muslims. The nature of the schematic diagram suggests a tenth- or eleventh-century prototype. A second Samaritan example is a drawing (fig. 13), of indeterminate date, displaying many of the same features as the Torah case.

In chased metal upon the case, we find depicted a highly schematized version of the Tabernacle/Temple. An outer rectangular perimeter is demarcated with lines representing a columnar structure. Within this framework are lines suggesting walls and small cell-like rooms, establishing an inner structure. Finally, another smaller rectangle can be seen with the Holy-of-Holies and its forechamber. In the *Sancta Sanctorum* we can discern the ark flanked by two tree-like rods; perhaps the rods of Moses and Aaron or Tree of Life symbols. Again, as in the Leningrad Bible fragment there are numerous other cult objects in the diagram, but they do not impinge upon our problem.

The Samaritan drawing is clearly a compilation of numerous elements, probably taken from various sources. Recognizable among them are the ark, upon which are two bird-like cherubim, two tree-like forms flanking the ark—*menorah*, scepter or Tree of Life symbols?[26] Below, in the next register, the *menorah* flanked by the table of the showbread on the left and the altar of incense on the right, and below these, a host of additional liturgical objects including the silver trumpets and the *shofar*.[27]

The unifying quality in the Leningrad Bible and the Samaritan examples, only three from many of this type, is the diagrammatic, non-spatial schematism of the representations with their emphases upon the depiction of the cult objects. A type of ritualistic literalism appears to be at the root of this form of illustration—a form which can perhaps be associated with an earlier Syro-Palestinian tradition.

This group of Temple/Tabernacle representations stands in sharp contrast to an illumination in a Greek Psalter of the mid-ninth century (fig. 14). Folio 165 recto of a monastic psalter, now preserved at Mount Athos, commands our attention. In the margin of Psalm 113 we find two different sets of images. In the lower margin we see three figures: the central figure crowned and bearded is David. To his right, a standing figure near two idols on stands, has been identified as John the Grammarian, a leader of the Iconoclasts. The other figure is labelled Bezalel, the builder of the Tabernacle. The Tabernacle itself is depicted in the right hand margin.[28]

Among the questions this illustration gives rise to is the relevance of the component parts to the text itself. Only verse 12 of the Psalm provides a text which can be related to the miniature: "The idols of the Gentiles are silver and gold, the works of the hands of men." In this context, we can understand the figure identified as John the Grammarian. This illustration, the product of post-iconoclastic sentiment in the Byzantine world, very clearly indicates that John was unable to recognize false "idols of silver and gold" mentioned in the Psalm, hence, by inference unable to discern the true images venerated by the iconodules. The presence of David, the Psalmist, poses no problem. Bezalel and the Tabernacle can be construed as being shown to emphasize the contrast between the idols of John and the true workmanship of God as manifest in the art of Bezalel. As related in Exodus 31.1-5,

> The Lord said to Moses, 'See, I have called by name Bezalel the son of Uri, son of Hur, of the tribe of Judah: I have filled him with the spirit of God, with ability and intelligence, with knowledge and all craftsmanship, to devise artistic designs, to work in gold, silver, and bronze, in cutting stones for setting, and in carving wood, for work in every craft.'

Thus Bezalel and the image of the Tabernacle stand as witness to the sanctity of God ordained images as distinct from the objects of John the Grammarian's iconoclasm.

The image of the Tabernacle itself is somewhat unusual, with aspects not readily explicable. In the central rectangle a table supports the ark, and above, the winged cherubim. Below, resting upon the lintel of the entrance are the *menorah* and an amphora. Between them is a three-legged table with tiny loaves of bread—the table of the showbread. The entire rectangle is surrounded by columns, extended from the center so as to create a larger rectangle around the Tabernacle itself. Protruding from the narrow end of this larger rectangle is a doorway hung with a curtain. The whole image is presented in a split perspective. The entire "plan" of the Tabernacle and the surrounding columnar court is literally "laid out," reminiscent of Egyptian spatial conventions, as in the wall paintings in the New Kingdom

Tomb of Rekh-mi-re, at Thebes.[29] But, the table, ark, and entrance are painted in a naturalistic, spatially conscious manner consonant with ninth-century Byzantine Hellenistic revival style. But more important for us is the strange attempt to accommodate the two different viewpoints—one spatially illusionistic, the other, diagrammatic. We find the same type of relationship between the similar components of the Codex Amiatinus plan. Further, it is by comparison with the Codex Amiatinus plan that we can arrive at a clearer understanding of the Mt. Athos Psalter illustration.

It is necessary at this point to go into a detailed analysis of the spatial conventions of the Amiatinus plan. Close observation reveals a treatment of the walls of the Tabernacle in a manner which suggests *both* the inner and outer surfaces. The artist shows a concern for the representation of space within the framework of illusionistic conventions, but at the same time is constrained by an earlier tradition which provided a more schematic view of the Tabernacle—the same tradition which dictated the extended, "laid-out" view of the perimeter columns. This architectural vision stands in sharp contrast to the famous Roman marble plan of the Porticus of Metullus, dating from the second century B.C.[30] The Roman plan employs a distinctly "modern" approach in its representation of columns and is quite distinct from the Egyptian example cited earlier or the Amiatinus plan. This observation aids in setting the Amiatinus plan outside the Roman tradition, and emphasizes Cassiodorus' debt to a Hellenistic source.

Returning now to the Mt. Athos Psalter: The combination of the liturgical elements—only the barest essentials—with a Tabernacle framed by the columnar perimeter, and the retention of the two different perspectives for plan and entrance, appear to me to indicate that the Mt. Athos illustration is an "abbreviation" of the type of illustration found in the Codex Amiatinus. As Kurt Weitzmann has pointed out, monastic psalters such as the one from Mt. Athos are paradigmatic of the migration of images from one textual source to a text of another type entirely.[31] Significantly, within this type of monastic psalter, there is frequently important marginal commentary upon the text, or illustrative material which supplements or replaces the written commentary. The latter is the case for the Mt. Athos illustration. I would suggest that the Codex Amiatinus illustration and the Mt. Athos illustration are both dependent upon and adapted from an earlier, illustrated manuscript of Egyptian Hellenistic origin. Of the two, the Codex Amiatinus example is closer, not only chronologically, but iconographically as well, to the prototype. This proposition can be supported by the close adherence of the Amiatinus miniature to the apocryphal texts cited earlier, and to the detailed indication of the disposition of the Hebrew tribes around the Tabernacle with the numbers of their force. Inasmuch as all of the additional information was quite meaningless for the context of the illustration in the Greek psalter, I would suggest that this abbreviated version was the resulting image.

The relationship of the Mt. Athos Psalter and the

Codex Amiatinus plan with the "constants" of the columnar perimeter "laid out" in the Egyptian mode, recalls the columnar perimeter around the Tabernacle on the Samaritan Torah case. In the Amiatinus and Mt. Athos versions the number of pertinent liturgical and cult vessels has been progressively reduced. On the other hand, in the type of representation found in the Leningrad Bible fragment, the cult objects become the main point of focus while all peripheral material is reduced.

Among the Samaritans, an age-old, persistent legend maintains that the Torah case we have been discussing is an exact representation of the Temple/Tabernacle with all of its attendant appurtenances. I would suggest rather, that the image on the Torah case represents the oldest extant tradition for Temple/Tabernacle depictions. I could not even begin to suggest a date for the origin of this tradition. Following from this archetype, the Codex Amiatinus reflects a prototype of Alexandrian Jewish origin, dating from the second or first centuries B.C. This date and provenance is arrived at because of the closeness of the Amiatinus plan to the apocryphal literature of this date and origin. In turn, the tradition represented by the Leningrad Bible represents another line of development from the archetype, but modified by the emphasis upon the liturgical vessels. I would suggest that this shift in emphasis may have occurred at the beginning of the third century of the Christian era, and possibly at Beth Shearim, in the Galilee—the time and place of the codification of the Jewish Oral Law—the *Mishnah*.[32]

From this preliminary investigation, **three patterns of**

illustration of Solomon's Temple during the Early Christian era begin to emerge. First, a narrative depiction representing the Temple, as exemplified by the painter's text in the Quedlinburg Itala, and possibly reflected in the illumination in the Roda Bible. I cannot, at this time, suggest a time or place of origin for this development. Second, the highly schematic, diagrammatic representations of the Temple/Tabernacle, with the emphasis upon the liturgical vessels and cult objects. This type is illustrated by the Leningrad Bible fragment, the Samaritan drawing, and any number of later examples from Hebrew Bibles of the thirteenth and fourteenth centuries.[33] This type of illustration may be based upon a Palestinian tradition of the third century A.D. And finally, the type of illustration represented by the Codex Amiatinus example. This last tradition, embodying a Hellenistic Jewish source of the second or first pre-Christian centuries, is one that loses its meaning and finds no continuation,[34] except in a manuscript such as the Mt. Athos psalter where it is taken out of context and abbreviated into an image which has no textual basis.

Thus for early Christianity we can say that the Temple of Solomon remained alive only as a thing of the heart and the spirit—a reality only as an inspiration to any who would emulate Solomon.[35]

1. C. Krinsky, "Representations of the Temple of Jerusalem before 1500," *Journal of the Warburg and Courtauld Institutes* 33 (1970), 1-7.

2. This approach is one developed and expanded through Early Christian and later Medieval art by P. Bloch, "Der Kirchenbau als neuer Tempel," *Monumenta Judaica, 2000 Jahre Geschichte und Kultur der Juden am Rhein, Handbuch* (Cologne, 1963), 756 ff. Other than what follows below, Bloch's material is beyond the scope of this paper.

3. Eusebius, *Ecclesiastical History* X, iv, 3-4, Loeb Classical Library (London, 1953), trans. J. E. L. Oulton, 399.

4. *Ibid.*, 413. Cf. R. Krautheimer, *Early Christian and Byzantine Architecture* (Baltimore, 1965), 78-79.

5. See the paper in this publication by Jean Ouellette.

6. Eusebius, *op. cit.*, 427.

7. Prudentius, *Lines to be Inscribed Under Scenes from History*, Loeb Classical Library II (London, 1953), trans. H. J. Thompson, 346-71.

8. C. Davis-Weyer, *Early Medieval Art, 300-1150* (Englewood Cliffs, 1971), 25.

9. Ill. in H. Woodruff, "The Illustrated Manuscripts of Prudentius," *Art Studies* 7 (1929), fig. 47.

10. A problem unto itself is the entire question of the Temple depictions in the wall paintings of the synagogue at Dura-Europos. It is important to note that in all of the architectural "temple" representations at Dura, it is only the presence of identifiable cult objects or labelled figures of Aaron and the priesthood which serves to distinguish a "Jewish Temple"

from a pagan one. They are all represented as the same architectural type.

11. H. Degering and A. Boeckler, *Die Quedlinburg Itala Fragmente* (Berlin, 1932), and more recently, I. Levin, *Itala Fragments* (Unpub. diss., New York University, 1971).

12. Degering and Boeckler, *loc. cit.*, 66 and *passim*: Davis-Weyer, *loc. cit.*, 24-25.

13. Cf. J. Dominguez-Bordona, *Spanish Illumination* I (Firenze, 1930), 30-1.

14. This area of speculation involves the continuity of a specifically Jewish illustrative tradition in Spain and the south of France, and is based upon a hypothesis, currently being worked upon by the author, concerning Jewish Old Testaments in Latin.

15. R. L. S. Bruce-Mitford, "The Art of the Codex Amiatinus," *The Journal of the British Archaeological Association* 3rd Ser., 32 (1969), 1-25.

16. *Ibid.*, 8.

17. Cassiodorus Senator, "Expositio Psalmorum," *Corpus Christianorum* Ser. Latina, 17, 18 (Turnholti, 1958).

18. *Ibid.*, Psalm 14, 11.38-41.

19. "The Sibylline Books," Bk. III, 11.24-6, in R. H. Charles, *The Apocrypha and Pseudepigrapha of the Old Testament* II (Oxford, 1969), 379.

20. "The Book of the Secrets of Enoch," 30:13, *idem.*, II, 499.

21. Charles, *op. cit.*, II, 370-1 and 425-9.

22. In his commentaries on Psalm 86 Cassiodorus quotes

extensively from Josephus' *Jewish Antiquities* VIII, 3, and in Psalm 14, *idem.*, III, 6. It is possible to interpret Cassiodorus' commentaries about Psalm 86 as referring to an image of the Temple which existed in the Josephus manuscript. (See note 23 below). I am grateful to Professor C. Reagan and Ms. Grace Houghton for this suggestion.

23. Although no early illustrated Josephus manuscripts are extant, Kurt Weitzmann [*Illustrations in Roll and Codex* (Princeton, 1970), 134] cites illustrations from the *Sacra Parallela* (Paris, Bib. Nat. cod. grec. 923) as evidence to adduce the existence of early illustrated Josephus manuscripts. In any case, we do know that Cassiodorus displayed a lively interest in Josephus' works as is manifested by his incorporation of the latter's *Antiquities* into his own *Historia tripartita*. Cf. L. W. Jones, *An Introduction to Divine and Human Readings by Cassiodorus Senator* (New York, 1969).

24. For this manuscript and bibliography see, T. Metzger, "Les objets du culte, le Sanctuaire du Désert et le Temple de Jérusalem dans les bibles hébraïques médiévales enluminées, en Orient et en Espagne," *John Rylands Library Bulletin* 52 (1969/70), 397-446; M. Metzger, "Quelques caractères iconographiques et ornementeaux de deux manuscrits hébraïques du Xe siècle," *Cahiers de civilisation médiévale* 1 (1958), 205-13.

25. For the Tree of Life see Z. Ameisenowa, "The Tree of Life in Jewish Iconography," *Journal of the Warburg and Courtauld Institutes* 2 (1938/39), 326-45.

26. This is seen in a variant form in Paris, Bib. Nat., ms. hébreu 7, fol. 12v. The iconographic interpretation of this and a related group of manuscripts depicting the Temple, Tabernacle and

Temple utensils is discussed by C. O. Nordström, "The Temple Miniatures in the Peter Comestor Manuscript in Madrid, "*Horae Soederblomianae* 6 (1964), 54-81, and reprinted in *No Graven Images*, ed. J. Gutmann (New York, 1971), 39-71.

27. For a discussion of the Samaritans and their cult objects see M. Gaster, *The Samaritans, Their History, Doctrines and Literature* [Schweich Lectures, London, British Academy, 1922 (Oxford 1925), esp. 193-4]; *idem., Hebrew Illuminated Bibles of the 9th and 10th Centuries* (London, 1901). The special significance of the liturgical utensils to the Samaritans is presented by M. F. Collins, "The Hidden Vessels in Samaritan Traditions," *Journal for the Study of Judaism* 3 (1972), 97-115. I would like to thank J. Gutmann for calling this article to my attention.

28. A complete discussion of this manuscript and its related monastic psalters can be found in S. Dufrenne, *L'illustration des psautiers grecs du Moyen Age* I (Paris 1966), esp. 34-5.

29. Ill. in N. deGaries Davies, *Paintings from the Tomb of Rekhmi-re* (Oxford, 1957), pl. 20.

30. Ill. in F. Brown, *Roman Architecture* (New York, 1965), pl. 14.

31. Weitzmann, *op. cit.*, 135 ff. and 148 ff.

32. See H. Danby, *The Mishnah* (Oxford, 1953).

33. For these manuscripts see Metzger, *loc. cit.*, and J. Gutmann, "When the Kingdom Comes," *Art Journal* 27 (1967/68), 168-75.

34. Two exceptions to this generalization are known to me: a plan

of the Tabernacle in a manuscript of Peter Comestor's *Histories* (Madrid, Bib. Nac., cod. res. 199, fol. 7v), discussed by Nordström, *loc. cit.* The other exception is in a Jewish manuscript in Florence (Laurentian Lib., Plut. III.10, fol. 95). The Madrid and Florence manuscript plans of the Tabernacle share the same spatial and perspective conventions and numerous iconographic features with the Codex Amiatinus plan. A colophon in the Florence manuscript has Alexandria as its place of origin (see: A. M. Biscioni, *Catalogus Bibliothecae Mediceo-Laurentianae* (Florence, 1752), 117 ff. However, most recently J. Gutmann ["Thirteen Manuscripts in Search of an Author: Joel ben Simeon, 15th Century Scribe-Artist," *Studies in Bibliography and Booklore* 9 (1970), 94, n. 27] has suggested quite convincingly that the Florence manuscript drawings were the product of a hand or workshop of fifteenth-century Northern Italy, close to the Jewish artist/scribe, Joel ben Simeon. Perhaps the colophon referring to Alexandria has some, still to be determined, relationship to the model, source or type behind the Florence manuscript depiction. Regardless of the provenance, the Madrid and Florence manuscripts attest to the longevity of a specific spatial convention and iconographic tradition related to illustrations of the Tabernacle.

35. I would like to thank Profs. Francois Bucher, James Marrow and Robin Oggins for their helpful suggestions, as well as Ms. Grace Houghton for her assistance. Prof. J. Gutmann, for inviting me to participate in this symposium and for his many useful suggestions deserves my special thanks.

SOLOMONIC ELEMENTS IN ROMANESQUE ART*

Walter Cahn

Of the three sanctuaries which successively stood on the traditional Mount Moriah, scarcely any vestige remained in view during the Middle Ages. The attention of travellers and pilgrims was in any case drawn with greater force to the Christian monuments of Jerusalem, those particularly associated with the events of the Passion of Christ: the Holy Sepulchre and the basilica of the Ascension first and foremost. Beginning in the middle of the ninth century, however, western Christianity came to identify the Muslim sanctuaries erected in the Temple precinct after the conquest of the Holy City by the Umayyads as of Solomonic authorship. These sanctuaries are the Dome of the Rock, completed in 691 by Caliph 'Abd al-Malik, and the Aqsa Mosque to the south, which was erected at the beginning of the eighth century, though thrice reconstructed in later times (fig. 15). Although these buildings are by no means identical in appearance with the Solomonic Temple as it is described in the Book of Kings, they were with some exceptions to overshadow entirely the word of Scripture in the consciousness of the Latin West until the reconstructions proposed in the sixteenth and seventeenth centuries, at the dawn of modern archaeology.

How this came to be so and how it affected representations of the Temple in Western Medieval art has been the subject of an excellent recent study by Carol Krinsky.[1] My own intention is to focus more narrowly on some aspects of the image of Solomon and the Temple in Romanesque art, here broadly taken to embrace the period from the eleventh to the early thirteenth century. This seems to me of particular interest since the Romanesque concern with Solomon was at once more intense and of a different quality than that of the earlier Middle Ages. The historical background is no doubt an important factor in this picture. When in 1099, the Crusaders conquered Jerusalem and established there the capital of the Latin Kingdom, the West came face to face for the first time with the structures which must heretofore have seemed more like a remote and exotic vision. The twelfth-century maps of Jerusalem constitute invaluable evidence for our perception of contemporary attitudes and appear in fact to have been the first cartographic depictions of the city in its entirety to have been made for western usage. I shall pass over the remarkable map of Cambrai, which gives the most accurate account of the topography, in favor of the more common type here represented by the twelfth-century Flemish exemplar in London (fig. 16) and known in a number of variant versions, which must all depend on a common model.[2] Jerusalem is in this view given a circular form and divided into four equal parts by intersecting streets marking the major areas. Upon this highly idealizing schema, which owes something to both

Roman methods of town planning and apocalyptic speculation, the principal landmarks have been superimposed, sometimes necessarily with a certain strain, but not in a totally arbitrary manner. The Solomonic structures straddle the upper two quadrants. They are the circular building of the Dome of the Rock, inscribed *Templum Domini*, and on the right side of the vertical axis, the Aqsa Mosque, shown as a basilica, and labelled *Templum Salomonis*. Below the latter edifice is an irregular enclosure lined with houses and inscribed *Claustrum Templi Solomonis*, or cloister of the Temple of Solomon. The area is accessible from the outer wall of the city through the *porta aurea*, which was held to be the gate traversed by Christ in his Entry into Jerusalem. The Cambrai map and some of the sources also designate the underground structures in the southern area of the Temple precinct as Solomon's stables (*stabula Salomonis*).

There are several aspects of this ensemble that are apt to be puzzling. The presence of not one but two temples no doubt reflects the existence on the site of the two Muslim shrines. But we can only ask why the difficulty of determining which was Solomon's was not resolved in favor of one or the other. Instead, the descriptions of the Holy Land seek to distinguish, in a somewhat tentative way, between first, a Temple of the Lord or Bethel constructed by Solomon on the threshing floor purchased by David and the site of Jacob's Vision of the Ladder, Christ's Presentation to the high Priest Simeon and Circumcision; and second, a

Temple of Solomon, also called in the sources a palace or porch erected by the same king. That this was not as troublesome at the time of the Crusaders as it is to us is almost certainly due to the fact that the coexistence side by side of two churches, one circular in plan and the other of the basilican type, was then something thoroughly familiar to everyone, since it represented the characteristic cathedral group as it had been known throughout the early Middle Ages. Such cathedral groups would include a major basilica and a building centralized in plan which might be either a baptistery or a church dedicated to the Virgin Mary. An episcopal chapel and palace, cloisters and houses for the canons could also be expected, as might a monumental gateway like the *porta aurea* where a bishop would make a ceremonial entrance.[3]

This reading of the monuments on the site of Solomon's Temple in light of the architectural experience of the time has yet another dimension. Although the historical associations, symbolism, no less than the intrinsic beauty of these monuments commended them to general attention, it would not have occurred to anyone to treat them as objects for detached contemplation. On the contrary, after the capture of Jerusalem, the Dome of the Rock was transformed into a church served by Augustinian Canons, and the Aqsa Mosque along with the surrounding site handed over to the Templars as the headquarters of their Order.[4] Some alterations were made within the mosque and other constructions were added, including a new church, cloisters and various storerooms and administrative buildings. It is no longer possible to gain an accurate picture of these additions, since they were probably demolished when Jerusalem was retaken by Salah al-Din in 1187 or in the successive occupations of the city in later times. But it is safe to say that the Temple site, like the Holy Sepulchre elsewhere in the city, did not present a fixed image to be passively recorded, but was itself gaining new features that could in turn be mirrored as Solomonic in the West.[5]

The cloister of the Temple of Solomon which is a conspicuous feature on the maps offers an example of this dynamic process. We do not know what topographic landmark stands behind the rubric on the maps. According to the description of the city by the German cleric Theoderich, the Templars "built a new cloister in the temple precinct in addition to the old one which they had in another part of the city."[6] Whether either of these is the cloister in question is uncertain at best. However, additional information regarding this construction is given by the writer known as Honorius of Autun, an author probably active in southern Germany who flourished in the first half of the twelfth century. In his treatment of function and significance of cloisters in church buildings, Honorius tells us that these are to be likened to the porch (*porticus*) built by Solomon near his Temple, and that this was the place where the apostles met after the Crucifixion to commune and pray.[7] The same view is expressed by two later writers on the symbolism of churches, Sicardus of Cremona in the thirteenth century[8] and Durandus of Mende in the fourteenth.[9] It may be that Honorius was alluding in this interpretation to depictions of the Descent of the Holy Spirit with the apostles shown within arcades, perhaps intended to suggest the *domus sapientiae* of Proverbs (9:1), an edifice said to have been supported by seven columns and thus capable of suggesting the image of a portico or cloister.[10] Be that as it may, Honorius' statement that the cloister of Solomon was the meeting place of the apostles has a much more graphic embodiment in a number of the cloisters erected in his time, where the apostles are represented as standing figures on the piers at the four corners. The earliest example known to us of this kind of arrangement is the cloister of Moissac in southern France, which, according to a reliable inscription, was completed in the year 1100, or only one year after the capture of Jerusalem by the Crusaders. In view of the short interval of time, it must seem doubtful that Moissac and other Romanesque cloisters with apostolic colleges have anything to do with developments in the Holy Land.[11] More likely, Honorius was moved to comment on an indigenous western development, which, I hasten to add, the Templars may very well have introduced into their cloister adjoining Solomon's alleged palace in Jerusalem. What we have here, then, is a Solomonic explanation or justification for an existing state of affairs, itself Solomonic in a much more remote or only symbolic sense.

A very explicit reference, this time to the biblical Temple of Solomon, is given by the pair of monumental columns of the cathedral of Würzburg (fig. 17). These columns were formerly part of the porch at the western portal of the cathedral, dismantled in 1644, and they are now to be seen in front of the baptismal chapel at the end of the southern aisle within the church.[12] Their capitals are respectively inscribed along the abacus *Iachim* and *Booz*, the names of the pillars which Solomon set up in front of his Temple. The style of the carving and of the epigraphy indicates a date near the beginning of the second quarter of the thirteenth century, and the columns are generally assumed to have come into being as part of the alterations and additions to the cathedral undertaken by Bishop Hermann of Lobdeburg, who ruled from 1225 to 1254. Hermann's predecessor had been a certain Theoderich, who is generally thought to be the figure of the same name who wrote a description of Jerusalem and of the Holy Land to which I have referred.[13] This description agrees on many points with the Holy Land itinerary of a somewhat earlier writer, John of Würzburg, who held a lesser clerical office in the same city. We have here perhaps a partial basis for the local interest in the Temple of Jerusalem.

Each of the two columns is composed of multiple shafts, bent and interpenetrating each other to form knots. *Booz* consists of a pair of shafts doubled and twice knotted with the help of an interloping strand in the middle. *Iachim* is made up of four thinner colonnettes doubled back and interwoven in the same way, but forming a single large knot at the center. Although the columns are to my knowledge unique in bearing Solomonic inscriptions, the remains of a column which must have been identical to our *Iachim* in the possession of the Hessisches Landesmuseum in Darmstadt would tend to indicate that such groups were once in wider currency (figs. 18-19).[14] Knotted columns employed in pairs as a motif of portal architecture are found at an earlier date in Italy, as, for example, in the portico of the central doorway of the cathedral of Ferrara, datable around 1135 (fig. 20).[15] In Italian Romanesque architecture, we also discover a number of other applications of the theme of the double columns flanking the entrance of a church. They may be free-standing, at some distance from the façade, as in the church of Sant' Agostino at Andria.[16] Or, they may be joined to the wall on each side of the portal, as at Santa Maria Maggiore in Tuscania. In these instances, it is not the presence of knots, but the gigantic scale of the columns, unrelated to any properly functional purpose, which sets them apart as exceptional and quasi-magical creations.

The origin and significance of the motif of the knotted columns is obscure. The earliest examples known to me are found in Byzantine book illumination of the eleventh century, as part of arcaded structures framing illustrations of the Gospels or Evangelist portraits, to which it would be hazardous to attribute a consciously symbolic intention.[17] I would like here to formulate the hypothesis that they may be derived from the ancient custom of tying cloth bands (*taeniae*) around free-standing columns which were commonly set up as cult symbols. Clement of Alexandria in his *Stromata* mentions such a column decorated with knotted bands in the shrine of Artemis on Argos, and such monuments can be seen in Pompeian frescoes.[18] It is to be expected that the custom, and indeed, the objects themselves, would not have survived the end of paganism. However, the antiquarian interests of the Macedonian Renaissance in the tenth century contributed to their reappearance in illuminated manuscripts. The depiction of David playing the harp in the company of a personification of Melodia in the famous Paris Psalter shows one of these columns very conspicuously marking the site as sacred ground (fig. 21).[19] But this is perhaps no more than the starting point for the idea of associating knot and column. The next step which is of particular interest to us is the idea of grouping knotted columns in pairs, as part of an architectural frame or canopy for a scene invested with special significance. As has been noted, it is first encountered in book illumination of the Comnenan period, and perhaps with most conspicuous effect in the Ascension miniature of the twelfth-century copy of the Homilies of James of Kokkinobaphos in Paris, set in what is regarded as a depiction of the Church of the Holy Apostles in Constantinople, founded by Justinian (fig. 22).[20] The iconostasis of Nerezi in Yugoslavia, dated 1164, shows a pair of such columns flanking the central doorway, while the images of Christ and of the Virgin Mary mounted in the lateral intercolumniations are framed by arches themselves sustained by pairs of knotted columns.[21] A most beautiful illustration of the same idea is found on a relief of the second quarter of the thirteenth century in the atrium of the Duomo at Spalato.[22] Here, we see the Annunciation set within a triple arcade with, at the center, the representation of an altar, candles and a chalice, no doubt intended to call to mind through the sacrifice of the Mass, the mystery of the Incarnation. We have here also in representational form the very definite association of the knotted columns with a sanctuary space. And from this, it must have been only a short distance to the idea of identifying such columns with the Temple of Solomon, as was done in the Würzburg portico.

But once again, the distance does not necessarily seem to have been negotiated in the most direct way, and the possible role of Holy Land models deserves to be investigated. Much of the work carried out by the Crusaders in the area of the Temple has, of course, been dismantled. But some columns and other fragments of carved stone were preserved and reemployed in the Aqsa Mosque and in the Dome of the Rock. Among these, there are several sets of twisted and knotted columns of various kinds, that are now incorporated into the structure of prayer niches and other decorative enclosures.[23] It has been possible to identify the source of one such set of columns now found in one of the galleries of the Dome of the Rock. They are the remains of the tomb of the young King Baldwin V, who died in 1186, just one year before the fall of the city to the Muslims, as it is known to us through an engraving made at the beginning of the nineteenth century (fig. 23, right).[24] These columns are of a braided type, with the coupling between the two paired shafts accomplished by means of loosely joined strands. Another set of columns reemployed in the Aqsa Mosque in which the shafts are twisted around one another possibly stems from the Templars' cloister (fig. 23, left).[25] In both cases as in the sculpture of the Latin Kingdom generally, we are dealing with a loose amalgam of Byzantine and Romanesque styles, and both types of columns can be discovered in the Latin West at a date almost certainly earlier than in the Holy Land, the twisted type in the cloister of Aix-en-Provence, for example, and the braided type on the façade of the church of St. Lazare at Avallon (fig. 24).[26] What the export of these inventions to the Holy Land contributed to them was a dimension of prestige and authority which could commend them, in the absence of any other form of guidance from tradition, as the most trustworthy relics of the Temple.

The spiralling columns of the Aqsa Mosque must surely call to mind the much better known Solomonic columns of St. Peter's in Rome.[27] The eleven columns of St. Peter—there were originally twelve—are likely works of Greek and possibly of Constantinopolitan origin, datable in the period from the middle of the second to the early years of the third century. According to the *Liber Pontificalis*, six were given to the church by Constantine, and the remaining were a present of the Byzantine Exarch to Gregory III (731-41). In the Renaissance, however, they were commonly believed to have come from the Temple of Solomon, and were so represented in depictions of the interior of the structure. When this notion first made its appearance is uncertain. It was unknown to the author of the *Mirabilia* and still to Petrus Mallius, writing under Alexander III, who died in 1181. During the Middle Ages, and possibly as part of the Proto-Renaissance currents around the year 1200, several copies were executed in the region between Rome and Naples.[28] The fact that these copies involve in each instance sets of two columns is perhaps not solely to be ascribed to economy and might well betoken the onset of a new, biblically-oriented interpretation. However this may be, the evidence available to us in which the columns of St. Peter's are identified with Solomon's Temple do not antedate the second half of the fourteenth century.[29]

This brief discussion of certain aspects of the role of the Temple in Romanesque art should now lead us to several observations of a more general nature on the subject. It is at the outset striking that the manifestations of Solomonic influence to which we can point are at once very literal and very limited in their scope. Literal in the sense that they aim to precisely reproduce or impersonate particular features of Solomon's Temple; limited in that they do not go beyond such particular features to a reconstruction of the larger whole. We have in the seven-branched candelabrum of Essen Minster a remarkable attempt to manufacture a replica of the *menorah*,[30] and in Rainier of Huy's font in Liège, an impressive reconstruction of the molten sea of Solomon's

Temple.³¹ But like the Würzburg *Iachim* and *Booz* and the copies of the twisted columns of St. Peter's, they were isolated elements in a setting that did not aim at an equally conscientious reconstruction of the entire Temple. These Romanesque objects have thus the quality of relics of the saints, which, though fragmentary, have the capacity of embodying the physical presence and moral authority of the whole person. And this desire to possess a material token of the Temple could extend to the person of the builder himself, for the monks of Saint-Denis believed themselves to possess in the beautiful Sasanian dish in their Treasure, Solomon's cup.³²

In the contemporary literature, a builder was sometimes held up to admiration as a new Solomon and an architect as a new Bezalel. These are conventional terms of flattery which need not and almost certainly did not imply any visible connection of the work in question and the biblical model or its later Islamic embodiment. It does seem to me of some significance that the persons addressed in this way were more often than not laymen—princes or lesser nobility commended for their patronage of a church or their foundation of a palace chapel.³³ It was their social status and their actions as munificent entrepreneurs that made them comparable to Solomon, not the design of the buildings which they erected. The sources also compel us to take note of a larger question raised by the use of the Temple as a model. No doubt, there existed a body of early medieval allegorical interpretation of the pertinent passages in the

Book of Kings representing the edifice as an image of the universal church.³⁴ To this, Richard of Saint-Victor's Commentary on the Temple of Solomon was to add a literal interpretation of the text and the same author's Commentary on Ezekiel's vision of the temple in the new Jerusalem went further to provide diagrams of the edifice as he imagined it.³⁵ Still, the Temple was bound to remain a distant and impractical dream once the threshold between imaginative speculation and practical planning was to be crossed. How the architecture and ceremonial vessels could be adapted to current liturgical usage is only the most obvious difficulty, even if Solomon's molten sea could suggest itself as a baptismal font. There was also the not negligible matter of expense: Abbot Suger of Saint-Denis in his description of the consecration of his new church claims with pride, but also, one gathers, with a certain touch of wistfulness, that he could not have completed his narthex without divine help, just as Solomon's riches would not have sufficed for his Temple.³⁶ Bernard of Clairvaux goes further in this direction to castigate luxury in monastic churches with the claim that such is the custom of the Jews, seemingly taking the Temple as the target for his scorn.³⁷ There remained for less rigorous minds the more diffuse but persistent image of a fabulous creation, which could only be incompletely perceived, and only duplicated piecemeal.

*Save for a few small emendations and the addition of notes, the text of this paper is that read at the Society for Biblical Literature meeting in Chicago. For a number of additional references, I am indebted to Professors Carol Krinsky and Joseph Gutmann.

1. C. H. Krinsky, "Representations of the Temple of Jerusalem before 1500," *Journal of the Warburg and Courtauld Institutes* 33 (1970), 1-19. On the theme generally, see also P. Bloch, "Nachwirkungen des Alten Bundes in der christlichen Kunst," *Monumenta Judaica* (Exh. Catal., Cologne, 1963), *Handbuch*, 735-81, especially 756ff., and R. Haussherr, "Templum Salomonis und Ecclesia Christi. Zu einem Bildvergleich der *Bible moralisée,*" *Zeitschrift für Kunstgeschichte* 31 (1968), 101-21.

2. The Cambrai map has been the subject of a recent analysis by L. H. Heydenreich, "Ein Jerusalem-Plan aus der Zeit des Kreuzfahrers," *Miscellanea pro arte. Hermann Schnitzler zur Vollendung des 60 Lebensjahres* . . . (Düsseldorf, 1965), 83-90. On the maps generally, see B. Röhricht, "Karten und Pläne zur Palästinakunde aus dem 7. bis 16. Jahrhundert," *Zeitschrift des Deutschen Palästina-Vereins* 14 (1891), 8-11, 87-92, 137-141; 15 (1892), 34-39, and the same author's comprehensive bibliography, *Bibliotheca Geographica Palaestinae*, ed. D. W. K. Amiram (Jerusalem, 1963), 598-662. W. Müller, *Die Heilige Stadt. Roma Quadrata, himmlische Jerusalem und die Mythe vom Weltnabel* (Stuttgart, 1961), 54ff. Z. Vilnay, *The Holy Land in Old Prints and Maps* (Jerusalem, 1963).

3. On early Medieval cathedral groups, see J. Hubert, *L'art préroman* (Paris, 1938), 38ff., and E. Lehmann, "Die frühchristlichen Kirchenfamilien der Bischofssitze im deutschen Raum und ihre Wandlung während des

Frühmittelalters," *Beiträge zur Kunstgeschichte und Archäologie des Frühmittelalters. Akten zum VII. Internationalen Kongress für Frühmittelalterforschung*, 21-28 Sept. 1958 (Graz-Cologne, 1962), 88ff.

The Golden Gate has been studied by J. Morgenstern, *The Gates of Righteousness* (Cincinnati, 1929) [reprinted from *Hebrew Union College Annual* 6]; see also most recently S. H. Steckoll, *The Gates of Jerusalem* (New York-Washington, 1968), 30ff. It might be useful to investigate, as a possible reflection of this toponym, its application to monumental entrances in western medieval architecture, as, for example, the west portal of Le Puy Cathedral, known in the sources as *porta aurea* [G. and P. Paul, *Notre-Dame du Puy. Essai historique et archéologique* (Le Puy, 1950), 106-107 and my monograph, *The Romanesque Wooden Doors of Auvergne* (New York, 1974), 2ff.]. A similar question might be raised in connection with the term *porta regia* or its romance equivalents, as for example, in the Portail Royal of Chartres Cathedral or the portal on the south side of the Cathedral of Modena (Porta Regia).

4. The Dome of the Rock was given to the Augustinian Canons in 1099 by Godefroy de Bouillon. They restored it and built a monastery and a cloister to the north of the monument. The Aqsa mosque was given by King Baldwin to the Templars Hugh of Payens and Geoffrey de Saint-Omer in 1118 (William of Tyre, *Histoire des Croisades*, ed. M. Guizot II (Paris, 1824), 203-205, and C. Enlart, *Les monuments des croisés dans le Royaume de Jérusalem. Architecture religieuse et civile* (Paris, 1925-28), 209.

5. On the topography of Jerusalem during the Latin Kingdom, see the surveys of Enlart, *op. cit.*, and T. S. R. Boase, *Castles and Churches of the Crusading Kingdom* (Oxford, 1967), 16ff.

6. Quoted from the translation of A. Stewart in the edition of the *Palestine Pilgrims Text Society* V (London, 1896), 31.

7. Honorius, *Gemma animae* (*P.L.* 172, 590): "Claustralis constructio juxta monasterium est sumpta a porticu Salomonis constructa juxta templum. In qua apostoli omnes unanimiter commanebant, et in templo ad orationem conveniebant, et in multitudini credentium cor unum et anima una erat, et omnia communia habebant." This text is discussed by W. Dynes "The Medieval Cloister as Portico of Solomon," *Gesta* 10 (1973), 61-70, and by L. Pressouyre, "St. Bernard to St. Francis: Monastic Ideals and Iconographic Programs in the Cloister," *idem*, 74.

8. Sicardus, *Mitrale* (*P.L.* 213, 25): "Claustrum ab excubiis, et custodiis Levitarum circa tabernaculum, vel ab atrio sacerdotium, vel a porticu Salomonis ad templum sumpsit exordium . . . Salomon vero fecit atrium sacerdotium, fecit et porticum quae patres militantis Ecclesiae repraesantabat antiquos, Abel et Enoch. In hac porticu apostoli commanentes unanimiter at orationem surgebant, et erat illis cor unum et anima una, quam formam canonici regulares et monachi arctius promittentes sequuntur, dum unanimiter in claustro . . ."

9. Durandus, *Rationale divinorum officiorum* I, 1, 42, a paraphrase of Sicardus' text. I have consulted the Antwerp edition (1570), 8.

10. See the material discussed by P. Bloch, "Ekklesia und Domus Sapientiae. Zur Ikonographie der Pfingst-Retabel im Cluny Museum," *Judentum im Mittelalter* (Berlin, 1966), 370-81.

11. M. Schapiro, "The Romanesque Sculpture of Moissac. I," *Art Bulletin* 13 (1931), 257f., and for the southern French cloisters generally, R. Rey, "L'art des cloîtres romans. Etude

iconographique," *Mémoires de la Société archéologique du Midi de la France* 23 (1955). Such apostolic colleges are especially frequent in Provence and the Rhône Valley, with representations at Saint-Trophîme in Arles, Notre-Dame des Doms in Avignon (single column with applied figure remaining), Aix-en-Provence, and Saint-Donat-sur-l'Herbasse [H.-A. von Stockhausen, "Die romanischen Kreuzgänge der Provence, II. Die Plastik," *Marburger Jahrbuch für Kunstwissenschaft* 8-9 (1936), 89-171]. A pier with apostles in relief from the cloister of Saint-Martin de Savigny [Cahn, *Gesta* 6 (1967), No. 1, 46-47]. In connection with the cloister of Moissac, it has been suggested that the presence of the apostolic college should be related to the influence of reforming ideals, stressing the return to the communal life shared by the apostles (M. Durliat, "Les origines de la sculpture romane à Toulouse et à Moissac," *Cahiers de civilisation médiévale* 12 (1969), 359, with reference to M.-R. Vicaire, *L'imitation des apôtres. Moines, chanoines et mendiants (IVe-XIIIe siècles)* (Paris, 1963).

12. C. Pöhlmann, "Der Dom zu Würzburg," *Archiv des historischen Vereins von Unterfranken und Aschaffenburg* 30 (1887), 289ff. F. Mader, *Die Kunstdenkmäler des Königreichs Bayern*, III, Heft 12. *Stadt Würzburg* (Munich, 1915), 40. The height of the columns is given as 2.45m by Pöhlmann, 2.50m by Mader. On their original position in the portal complex of the cathedral, I have followed the remarks of Pöhlmann, though a new study is clearly required.

13. Theoderich von Hohenburg or Homburg an der Wern is mentioned as bishop of Würzburg between 1223 and 1225 [A. Amrhein, "Reihenfolge der Mitglieder des Adeligen Domstiftes zu Würzburg," *Archiv des historischen Vereins von Unterfranken und Aschaffenburg* 33 (1889), 321].

14. M. Fath, "Katalog der Architekturfragmente im Hessischen Landesmuseum in Darmstadt," *Kunst in Hessen und am Mittelrhein* 10 (1970), 123, Nos. 18 (base and quadruple shaft) and 19 (carved knot). The capital is said to be in Dieburg Museum. After the above was written, two other monuments with Solomonic columns came to my attention. The pair of columns which frame the triumphal arch at the entrance of the choir of the church of Champeix in Auvergne bear foliate capitals whose imposts are inscribed with the names CIACHIN and BOOT [Z. Swiechowski, *Sculpture romane d'Auvergne*, (Clermont-Ferrant, 1973), 33-34]. Professor Gutmann has also pointed out to me the inscription (I Kings 7:41ff.) of one of the columns in the synagogue of Worms, which alludes to the pillars of the Temple. The numerical value of the Hebrew corresponds to the year 1174-75, marking the rebuilding of the structure [O. Böcher, *Die alte Synagoge zu Worms. Der Wormsgau*, Beiheft 18 (Worms, 1960), 101-103].

15. T. Krautheimer-Hess, "Die figurale Plastik der Ostlombardei von 1100-1178," *Marburger Jahrbuch für Kunstwissenschaft* 4 (1928), 255ff. In addition to the (not wholly accurate) list of knotted columns given by Pöhlmann, *loc. cit.*, the following examples can be cited. Although not designed to constitute a comprehensive list, they show the motif to have been diffused in Italian art and in Germany, probably under Italian influence. 1. S. Quirico d'Orcia, portal flanked by knotted columns supported by lions [M. Salmi, *Chiese romaniche della Toscana* (Milan, 1961), 115]. 2. Cathedral of Embrun (Alpes-Maritimes), single quadruple shaft engaged in the porch [Y. Christ, *Cathédrales de France* (Paris, 1950), 39, pl. 100]. 3. Abbey of Chiaravalle, cloister [*Lombarda Occidentale, Touring Club Italiano* (1956), 187]. 4. Gropina, (Tuscany) support of a pulpit [W. Biehl, *Toskanische Plastik*

des frühen und höhen Mittelalters (Leipzig, 1926), 29]. 5. Campiglia Marittima, Pieve di S. Giovanni, fragment [P. Bacci, "La Pieve di San Giovanni a Campaglia Marittima, costruito de Maestro Matteo," *Rivista d'arte* (1910), 53]. 6. San Marco, Venice, Porta S. Alippio [O. Demus, *The Church of San Marco in Venice* (Washington, 1960), pl. 88]. 7. Wimpfen, Kaiserpfalz [A. Heckel, *Der Runde Bogen*, Blaue Bücher (Königstein im Taunus, 1957), 9]. 8. Rhenish ivory, Karlsruhe, Badisches Landesmuseum, No. 60/53 [*Jahrbuch der Staatlichen Museen in Baden-Württemberg* 1 (1964), No. 33, 49-50].

16. A. Blunt, "The Temple of Solomon with Special Reference to South Italian Baroque Art," *Kunsthistorische Forschungen. Otto Pächt zu seinem 70. Geburtstag* (Vienna, 1972), 258-65.

17. Gospels, Venice, Bib. Naz. di San Marco, gr. 540, fol. 14 [H. Buchthal, *Miniature Painting in the Latin Kingdom of Jerusalem* (Oxford, 1957), 4, and pl. 142c]. Gospels, Oxford, Bodleian Auct. t infra I, 10, fols. 16v, 178v [C. Meredith, "The Illustration of the Codex Ebnerianus," *Journal of the Warburg and Courtauld Institutes* 29 (1966), 419-24]. Gospels, Messina, Bib. Univ. F. S. Salvatore 88 [F. Daneu Lattanzi, *Lineamenti di storia della miniature in Sicilia* (Florence, 1968), fig. 13]. The knot represented—our square knot— is the *nodus Herculis*, which was believed in Antiquity to possess magic beneficient powers [see C. L. Day, *Quipus and Witches' Knots. The Role of the Knot in Primitive and Ancient Cultures* (Lawrence, Kan., 1967), 53ff.].

18. W. Haftmann, *Das italienische Säulenmonument* (Leipzig and Berlin, 1939), 7. See also the article "Taenia" in Pauly-Wissowa-Kroll, *Real-Encyclopädie der classischen Altertumswissenschaft*, Ser. 2, VIII, 2002-2006. For a

selection of representations in ancient art, see G. E. Rizzo, *La pittura ellenistica-romana* (Milan, 1929), pls. LXIV, CVIII, CXVIII and CLXXII.

19. Bibl. Nat. gr. 139, fol. 1. H. Buchthal, *The Miniatures of the Paris Psalter* (London, 1938), 13ff. The appearance of such columns in an illustrative context seems exceptional in Byzantine art, though we observe the motif again in a thirteenth-century copy of the miniature in Leningrad, Public Library Cod. 269 [K. Weitzmann, "Eine Pariser Psalter-Kopie des 13. Jahrhunderts auf dem Sinai," *Jahrbuch der österreichischen byzantinischen Gesellschaft* 6 (1957), 129 and pl. 3].

20. Bibl. Nat. gr. 1208, fol. 2v. R. Krautheimer, "A Note on Justinian's Church of the Holy Apostles in Constantinople," *Mélanges Eugène Tisserant* II (Vatican City, 1964), 265-70 [reprinted in the same author's *Studies in Early Christian, Medieval and Renaissance Art* (London-New York, 1969), 197-201] has argued that the miniature reveals a rebuilding of Justinian's church in the second third of the tenth century. He does not indicate whether the knotted columns should be taken as a part of the original edifice, the middle Byzantine rebuilding, or indeed, whether the miniature reflects the situation accurately on this point.

21. See the reconstruction in A. Grabar, *L'art de la fin de l'antiquité et du moyen âge* I (Paris, 1968), 410 and pl. 107c.

22. P. Toesca, *Storia dell'arte Italiana. Il Medioevo* II (Turin, 1927), 800.

23. Boase, *op. cit.*, 19.

24. J. Strzygowski, "Ruins of the Tombs of the Latin Kings," *Speculum* 11 (1936), 499-508.

25. See the reproduction in *Jerusalem. A History*, ed. J. Boudet (New York, 1967), 219.
26. For Aix, see Stockhausen, *op. cit.*, 135ff. For Avallon, J. Vallery-Radot, "L'iconographie et le style des trois portails de Saint-Lazare d'Avallon," *Gazette des Beaux-Arts* 52 (1958), 23-34. Braided columns are seen also in Byzantine art, as on the ivory casket with the Ascension of Alexander in Darmstadt [*Die Sammlungen des Baron von Hüpsch* (Darmstadt-Cologne, 1964), No. 2].
27. J. B. Ward-Perkins, "The Shrine of St. Peter and its Twelve Columns," *Journal of Roman Studies* 42 (1952), 21-33.
28. E. Mauceri, Colonne Tortili cosi dette del Tempio di Salomone," *L'arte* 1 (1898), 377-81, and Ward-Perkins, *op. cit.*, 27ff. The date of these copies has not yet been firmly established. Ward-Perkins considers the set formerly in Santa Chiara in Naples to be of ancient origin, and the pair of columns of SS. Trinita dei Monti in Rome and San Carlo at Cave di Palestrina to have been executed some time after the eighth century. On the other hand, H. Wentzel, "Antiken-Imitationen des 12. und 13. Jahrhunderts in Italien," *Zeitschrift für Kunstwissenschaft* 9 (1955), 55ff., seems to place the entire group, though without detailed analysis, into the Romanesque period. A pair of twisted columns which appears to represent still another set of Medieval copies is illustrated in a sales catalogue of 1949. Its present whereabouts is not known to me [*Classical and Medieval Stone Sculpture . . . Part III of the Joseph Brummer Collection*, Parke-Bernet Galleries (New York, 1949), 158, No. 633; here described as "Veneto-Byzantine" and dated ca. XIIth century]. The set of columns at San Carlo in Cave are inscribed **MARMOREAE COLUMNAE SALOMONICA**

TEMPLI, but the character of the epigraphy, judging from the reproduction in the above cited article of Mauceri, indicates a Renaissance date.

29. As far as I have been able to establish, the earliest author to associate at least one of the columns of St. Peter's with the temple of Solomon is the anonymous author of the *Memoriale de mirabilibus et indulgentiis quae in urbe Romana existunt* (R. Valentini and G. Zucchetti, *Codice topografico della citta di Roma* IV (Rome, 1940-53), 81. The writer, a Benedictine monk, is thought to have been active during the reigns of Urban V (1362-70) or Gregory IX (1370-78). He ascribes a Solomonic origin to the *colonna santa*, against which Christ is said to have leaned when he preached: "Item in dicta ecclesia est una columpna alba, sculpta, circumsepta rexiis ligneis, quae antiquitus fuit portata de Iherusalem de templo Solomonis, super quam recubuit Christus, quando praedicabat; cuius virtute demoniati eam amplectenter curantur ut vidi." In John of Capgrave's *Ye Solace of Pilgrims* (Valentini-Zucchetti, *op. cit.*, 335-36), the same story is told, but with the significant addition of the other columns to the list: "This is the pilere on whech our Lord Ihesu Crist lened whann he preched to the people and on whech he rested whann he prayed to the Fader in hevene, which pilere with other .XI. that stande her a bout were brout fro Salomones temple on to this nobel cherch..." Capgrave's work is dated by his editors between 1450 and 1453. M. Cerrati, *Tiberii Alpharanii De Basilicae Vaticanae ... structura* (Studi e Testi, XXVI, Rome, 1914) 53ff., who discusses this question indicates only that the story of the Solomonic origin of the columns is late in date and of popular origin. On the *colonna santa*, see also A. Busiri-Vici, *La "colonna santa" del tempio di Gerusalemme* (Rome, 1888).

It may also be appropriate to mention in this context the four bronze columns now part of the altar of the Holy Sacrament in San Giovanni in Laterano [S. Ortolani, *S. Giovanni in Laterano, Le chiese di Roma illustrate*, 13 (Rome, s.d.), 56] which are also said to have come from the temple of Solomon. The *Liber Pontificalis* credits Sergius III (904-11) with having donated these to the church (Valentini-Zucchetti, *op. cit.*, III, 331) but without indication of their provenance. The idea that they stem from the Temple in Jerusalem is again found in the *Memoriale de mirabilibus*: "Item sunt ante altare ipsius ecclesiae quatuor columpnae cuprae, quarum longitudo .XXX II. palmi, et grossitudo .X. et plus, cum capitellis cupreis, inferioribus et superioribus. Et fuerunt deportatae de templo Salomonis per Constantinum imperatorem." (*Ibid*, IV, 85-86). The Lateran columns are also mentioned in the itinerary of the twelfth-century traveler, Benjamin of Tudela, ed. A. Asher I (New York, 1840), 40, where a Solomonic origin is already ascribed to them: "In St. Giovanni in Laterano ... there are two copper pillars constructed by King Schlomo o.b.m. whose name Schlomo ben David is engraved upon each."

Finally, it may be of interest to cite the curious passage in the twelfth-century *De mirabilibus urbis Romae* of Master Gregory (*ibid*, III, 154), where the two reclining figures of bearded antique divinities now in front of the Senatorial Palace on the Campidoglio are respectively interpreted as Solomon and Pope Liberius: "Harum alteram Salomonis effigiem dicunt, alteram vero Libero Patris ymaginem asserunt."

30. P. Bloch, "Siebenarmige Leuchter in christlichen Kirchen," *Wallraf-Richartz Jahrbuch* 23 (1961), 55-190.

31. See on the font most recently the Exhibition Catalogue *Rhein und Maas* (Cologne, 1972), 238-39, No. G 1.

32. The plate of Chosroes II was given to Saint-Denis by Charles the Bald. Neither Suger nor his biographer William have anything to say about it, but the connection with Solomon is made in the earliest inventory of the treasure of Saint-Denis which we possess, compiled in 1505. See H. Omont, "Inventaire du trésor et des objets précieux conservés dans l'église de Saint-Denis en 1505 et 1739," *Mémoires de la Société de l'histoire de Paris et de l'Ile-de-France* 28 (1901), 173: "Une tasse d'or, qu'on disoit le plat Salomon . . ." See also the commentary of M. Conway, "The Abbey of Saint-Denis and its Ancient Treasure," *Archaeologia* 16 (1914-15), 121.

33. The following is a selection of cases: 1. Panegyric of Eusebius on the construction of the basilica in Tyre [*Eccles. Hist.*, X, iv, 3-4; Loeb Classical Library (1938), 388-89]. This reference is unusual in that the addressee is a bishop, but Eusebius is quite aware of the difficulty since he wonders "whether one should call thee a new Bezalel, the architect of a divine tabernacle, or Solomon . . . or even a Zerubbabel." 2. Justinian exclaims on the completion of the Hagia Sophia: "Solomon, I have surpassed thee." The story is recorded in the so-called Anonymous Account, datable not earlier than the twelfth century [W. R. Lethaby and H. Swainson, *The Church of Sancta Sophia, Constantinople. A Study of Byzantine Building* (London-New York, 1894), 141, 144]. This work lists other sources in which the comparison of the building with the Temple, and of the builder with Solomon, are made: according to Glycas, Justinian set up a statue of Solomon looking at the church and gritting his teeth with envy, etc. . . . On the subject, see G. Scheja, "Hagia Sophia und Templum Salomonis," *Istanbuler Mitteilungen* 12 (1962), 44-58, who has marshalled the evidence in favor of an influence of the biblical description on the Justinianic structure. 3.

Charlemagne's Palatine Chapel at Aachen is compared to the Temple by Notker the Stammerer (*Gesta Caroli, M.G.H. Script*, II, 744), and Alcuin praises Charlemagne as another Solomon (cf. Bloch, *Nachwirkungen*, 769). 4. Einhard is praised as another Bezalel (*ibid.*), and later Thietmar, who assisted Poppo in the building of the church of Stavelot [V. Mortet, *Recueil de textes relatifs à l'histoire de l'architecture et à la condition des architectes en France* (Paris, 1911), 38, n. 2]. Rodolphus, a goldsmith who worked at Saint-Benoît-sur-Loire is similarly qualified (*idem*, 38). 5. William of Ypres, a nephew of the Count of Flanders, is qualified as another Solomon for his role in assisting abbot Leonius (1138-63) in various building enterprises at Saint-Bertin (*idem*, 120). 6. The chapel of the lords of Ardres, near Dunkirk, is praised for its resemblance to the tabernacle built by Solomon (*idem*, 185). One observes in the twelfth-century sources an appropriation of the flattering comparison with Solomon and his sanctuary on behalf of men not in the immediate circle of royalty. This is a phenomenon which has been discussed in a larger context by G. Duby, "Remarques sur la litterature généalogique en France aux XIe et XIIe siècles," *Comptes-rendus de l'Académie des Inscriptions et Belles-Lettres* (1967), 335-45.

Another aspect of the same process of appropriation is the representation of Solomon on Medieval buildings, which deserves more extended inquiry. See for example the relief, allegedly depicting Solomon, on the town hall of Saint-Antonin [R. Hamann-MacLean, "Das ikonographische Problem der 'Freiburger Jungfrau'," *Marburger Jahrbuch für Kunstwissenschaft* 10 (1937), 64-65, fig. 41], and the reference to a mosaic image of the king above the entrance of the Hagia Sophia, according to a fifteenth-century Russian traveller (Lethaby and Swainson, *op. cit.*, 110).

34. We may quote as a representative text Peter of Roissy, who states: "Ecclesia itaque figurata est in Templo Salomonis vel in tabernaculo Veteris Testamenti." (Mortet, *op. cit.*, 184, and on the author, M.-Th. d'Alverny, "Les mystères de l'église, d'après Pierre de Roissy," *Mélanges offerts à René Crozet* II (Poitiers, 1966), 1085-1104. There is a body of modern scholarship which proposes to comprehend Medieval architectural systems as reflections of the Temple of Jerusalem, understood either as the sanctuary of Solomon, or that envisioned by Ezekiel, or preferably, the eschatological vision of St. John in the Book of Revelations. The results appear to me limited, of necessity, to the broadest, not to say platitudinous, level of allusion. See for examples of this approach H. Sedlmayr's *Die Entstehung der Kathedrale* (Zurich, 1950); A. Stange, *Das frühchristliche Kirchengebäude als Bild des Himmels* (Cologne, 1950) and certain passages in Otto von Simson's *The Gothic Cathedral* (New York, 1956).

35. *P.L.* 196, 223-42 and 527-60. B. Smalley, *The Study of the Bible in the Middle Ages* (Oxford, 1952), 106ff. The diagrams are found in Bibl. Nat. lat. 14516, which I consider likely to be the original copy of the work. Later copies are found in Bodleian Library Mss. 494, 459 and e. Mus. 62 [O. Pächt and J. J. G. Alexander, *Illuminated Manuscripts in the Bodleian Library* III (Oxford, 1973), Nos. 185, 312 and 382]. I propose to devote a special study to these designs, which are also reproduced in the edition of the text in the Patrologia Latina.

36. *De consecratione*, in E. Panofsky, *Abbot Suger on the Abbey Church of St.-Denis and its Art Treasures* (Princeton, 1946), 90-91.

37. *Apologia ad Guillelmum, P.L.* 182, 914: The singular passage

is deserving of note: "Omitto oratorium immensas altitudines, immoderatas longitudines, supervacuas latitudines, sumptuosas depolitiones, curiosas depictiones: quae dum orantium in se retorquent aspectum, impediunt et affectum, et mihi quodammodo repraesentant antiquum ritum Judaeorum."

THE TEMPLE OF SOLOMON
IN ISLAMIC LEGEND AND ART

Priscilla Soucek

The Temple of Solomon and its legacy to Islamic civilization will be the subject of this inquiry. Three basic problems will be analyzed. The first will be to discover what information concerning the structure, location and decoration of the Solomonic Temple is preserved in Islamic sources. The second will be to investigate what importance, if any, knowledge of the Solomonic Temple had in the decision of the Caliph 'Umar ibn al-Khaṭṭāb to build the first mosque of Jerusalem on the southern side of the traditional Mt. Moriah near the present al-Aqṣā Mosque.[1] The role of Solomonic traditions in the construction of the first major monument of Islamic religious architecture, the Dome of the Rock, which was placed over the rock out-cropping traditionally associated with the Solomonic Temple, will also be considered.[2] The last subject to be discussed is the relationship of the traditions connected to the Temple with the complex group of legends surrounding the "Night Journey" (*Isrā'*) and "Ascension" (*Mi'rāj*) of the Prophet Muhammad.[3] According to presently accepted beliefs the Prophet's "Night Journey" was to Jerusalem, and it was from there that he ascended to Heaven.

I

Information concerning the Solomonic Temple is found in a variety of Islamic sources. On the simplest level, the construction of the Temple and its subsequent destruction were recognized as events of considerable importance. Mas'ūdī (d. c. 956) mentions the Temple as one of the three significant religious monuments of antiquity, the others being the Pyramids of Egypt and the Temple of Antioch.[4]

A further indication of the importance attached to the Temple by Islamic historians is found in the historical manual of Ibn Qutaybah (d. 889). Here the destroyer of the Temple Bukhtnaṣṣar, as Nebuchadnezzar was known in Islam, is named along with Nimrud as exemplifying rulers who were "Infidels." Conversely, Solomon and Alexander the Great are described as "True Believers."[5] The source of this tradition is given as Wahb b. Munabbih, a Yemenite convert to Islam probably of Jewish descent, who is often cited by early Islamic scholars as an authority on biblical traditions.[6]

Two early Islamic scholars concerned with the chronology of world history, Hamza Isfahānī (d. 961) and Abū Rayḥān al-Bīrūnī (d. c. 1051), give information concerning the dates of the construction and destruction of the Temple. In the system of Hamza Isfahānī the construction of the Temple is dated to 480 years after the Exodus while its destruction is placed at 890 years after the Exodus. Curiously he also uses the dates of the construction and destruction of the Temple in his calculations of the life of Alexander the Great. The assumption of power by Alexander is placed at 717 years after the construction of the Temple. Conversely the death of Alexander is located at 269 years after the destruction of the Temple by Bukhtnaṣṣar.[7]

Al-Bīrūnī uses the same figures for the dates of the construction and destruction of the Temple as Hamza Isfahānī, but decreases the interval between the reconstruction of the Temple and the advent of Alexander, so that the Alexandrian era begins exactly 1,000 years after the Exodus. Al-Bīrūnī also uses the dates connected with the Solomonic Temple in his computations of the date of the birth of Christ.[8]

While these references to the construction and destruction of the Solomonic Temple relate it to a system of world chronology, al-Bīrūnī also connects Alexander with the Temple, thereby continuing the parallelism between Solomon and Alexander implicit in the remarks of Ibn Qutayba and Hamza Isfahānī. According to al-Bīrūnī when Alexander had gained control over Greece and Egypt, he turned his attention to Jerusalem where he visited the Temple and made offerings. That Alexander's actions should be construed as respect for the Temple is further indicated by the reason given for his invasion of Iran. According to al-Bīrūnī the invasion was to avenge the injustice inflicted on Syria by Bukhtnaṣṣar, an apparent reference to the destruction of the Solomonic Temple.[9] The connection between Bukhtnaṣṣar and the Iranian rulers would appear to stem from a tradition which makes Bukhtnaṣṣar the envoy of an Iranian ruler, Luhrāsp.[10]

Al-Bīrūnī's most detailed discussion of the destruction of Solomon's Temple occurs in the section of his *Surviving Traces of Past Nations* (*Al-Āthār al-Bāqīya 'an al-Qurūn al-Khālīya*) which deals with Jewish religious holidays. Under the month of Āb, al-Bīrūnī mentions fasting on the 9th, 25th and 28th days of the month as connected with various aspects of the Temple's destruction. Of these the fasting on the 9th was the most important, for this day was held to commemorate the destruction and burning of the Temple by Bukhtnaṣṣar. Characteristically the second demolition is mentioned but the identity of the destroying army is not revealed. It, too, was remembered to have occurred on the 9th day of Āb.[11]

An illustration in the early fourteenth-century copy of al-Bīrūnī's text now in the University of Edinburgh Library gives a dramatic version of the Temple's demolition (fig. 25).[12] Since al-Bīrūnī specifies that Bukhtnaṣṣar's destruction of the city and Temple was accompanied by a conflagration, the painting appears to represent the destruction of the Solomonic Temple. Thus the figure standing at the right directing the men who are demolishing the structure must be Bukhtnaṣṣar himself. This artist's depiction of the Temple shows it as a large dome supported by a circular colonnade and enclosed by a wall. This structure is analogous to that of the Islamic shrine, the Dome of the Rock, which suggests that the fourteenth-century artist felt that the two buildings had a similar appearance.

The burning structure is identified by a white inscription repeated around the base of the dome which reads "Bayt al-Muqaddas" or "Bayt al-Maqdis." This name represents the Arabic form of the Hebrew name for the Temple. It was used in the Islamic world as the name of both the Temple proper and of the city of Jerusalem. This double usage created an ambiguity which was resolved in various ways. Al-Bīrūnī refers to the city as "Bayt al-Muqaddas" and to the Temple as "al-Bayt".[13]

While the references from Ibn Qutayba, Hamza Isfahānī and al-Bīrūnī suggest that the demolition of the Temple was viewed as an act of desecration, the Quranic allusion to the event has a different tone. The context of Sura 17 suggests that the destruction was a punishment to the Jews for disobeying the warnings of God. It was because of this:

> That they may enter the Temple (al-Masjid) as they entered it before; that they may destroy completely what they have seized.[14]

Since the verse stresses the severity of the second destruction of the Temple, it would appear to give less weight to the campaign of Bukhtnaṣṣar. However, the commentaries collected by Ṭabarī (d. 923) show that the traditions of the Solomonic Temple were more vividly remembered than those connected with the later structure. Thus it is the final destruction of the Temple which is associated with Bukhtnaṣṣar, not the first. The first destruction is described by one source as "only a raid."[15]

Most of the commentators do not specify the organizer of the first attack, although Sennacherib is mentioned by some.[16] The main emphasis is on the devastation caused by Bukhtnaṣṣar. The destruction of the building was said to be followed by the desecration of the site by dumping corpses and other refuse upon it.[17]

With respect to the name of the Temple, the Quranic term "al-Masjid" is usually explained as "Bayt al-Muqaddas" although one source calls it "Masjid Bayt al-Muqaddas," or "the Sanctuary of Bayt al-Muqaddas."[18]

While the Quranic citation of the Temple's destruction again puts the event in the larger context of world history, a remark in the *Kitāb Futūḥ al-Buldān*, "The Conquest of Territories," of Balādhurī (d. 892) suggests that the event was also remembered in Arabia at the time of the Prophet Muhammad. Balādhurī remarks that the Jews of Yathrib, as Medina was known before the arrival of the Muslim community in 622, had moved there after the destruction of "Bayt al-Muqaddas" by Bukhtnaṣṣar.[19]

From the information given above it is clear that for the Islamic community the construction and destruction of the Solomonic Temple were important events in the history of the pre-Islamic world. Although references exist to two phases of the Temple, it was the Solomonic Temple and its destruction by Bukhtnaṣṣar which had left the more lasting memories.[20]

In addition to discussing the destruction of the Temple, Islamic authors also deal with the significance of its location, the process of its construction and the decoration used to embellish the structure. With respect to the location of the building, Islamic authors assume that it was built around the rock formation which is presently enclosed by the Dome of the Rock.[21] The significance of the Temple site was also widely acknowledged. Underlying many of the traditions repeated by Islamic authors is the assumption that the vicinity of the Temple was of particular holiness. While the question of the evolution of traditions connected with the Temple area during the early Islamic period is very complex, evidence suggests that by the end of the first century of the Islamic era the Temple area was regarded as one of the holiest places in the world.[22]

As was the case with the destruction of the Temple, the notion of the sanctity of the area was thought to be reflected in certain Quranic phrases. The references to "the Holy Land" and "the land which we have blessed" figure in the discussions of the problem. Judging from the commentaries collected by Ṭabarī, the early tendency appears to have been to equate "the Holy Land" with the whole Syro-Palestinian area, while the phrase "the land which we have blessed" from Sura 21 verse 71 had apparently acquired a more particular significance.[23] Although some authorities tended to give the term a broad interpretation, the reputation of the Temple area as the scene of significant religious events appears to have encouraged a more specific interpretation of the phrase.

In the traditions quoted by Ṭabarī, the "blessings"

surrounding the Temple area, or "Bayt al-Muqaddas," are connected with its being the site of the gathering of mankind at the end of the world.[24] Another tradition connects the rock of the Temple with sweet water springs. One authority declares that this water is the "sweetest" in the world.[25]

While Ṭabarī's sources give glimpses of these traditions, the earliest systematic description of the various miracles and religious events connected with the Temple area is found in the *Kitāb al-Buldān*, a geographical treatise completed in the early years of the tenth century by Ibn al-Faqīh. The remarks collected in a section called "Bayt al-Muqaddas" deal with Quranic references to the site and to the many manifestations of its sanctity recorded in the past and predicted for the future.[26] On the authority of Muqātil ibn Sulaymān (d. circa 767) he associates the phrase "the land which we have blessed" with "Bayt al-Muqaddas."[27] The site is further characterized as the "first place" blessed by God as well as being the location of numerous divine revelations. Among the miracles of the pre-Islamic period associated with the site are: the dream of Jacob, the annunciation to Abraham of the impending birth of Isaac, the annunciation to Zachariah of the birth of John the Baptist, and the visit of angels to David.[28] The version of the founding of the Temple given by Ibn al-Faqīh emphasizes the hallowed nature of the location, thus using the general associations with the site to justify the construction of a sanctuary.[29]

The texts collected by Ibn al-Faqīh provide documentation for the popularity of the concept of the intrinsic sanctity of the Temple area, but other Islamic authors give a more historical version of the reasons for the selection of the site. For example, Ṭabarī offers two related explanations for the choice of the site. Both of them appear to contain echoes of the account contained in 2 Samuel 24. The simplest version states that during the reign of David a plague occurred among the people of Israel. The community went to the site of the future Temple and prayed for deliverance from this affliction. When their prayer was answered:

> they made that place into a Temple (*masjid*).[30]

The second version of the story is attributed to Wahb ibn Munnabih. In this version the plague was caused by David himself when he ordered a census taken of the people of Israel. Since the covenant of Abraham and Jacob had promised that their descendants would be "as numerous as the stars in the heaven" David's request was viewed as showing his lack of faith. As a punishment David was given three choices: the people of Israel would have to suffer three years of famine, three months of war or three days of death. Fearing the first two, David reluctantly agreed to the third. However, after one day of plague David was so horrified at the number of dead that he appealed to God to withdraw the punishment. When the prayer was answered David saw angels ascending a golden ladder from the rock to the sky, sheathing their swords as they went. From this he concluded:

> This is the place where a Temple (*masjid*) must be built.[31]

The two related accounts given by Ṭabarī show in a more limited way the theme of the intrinsic sanctity of the site of the future Temple. The theme of the angels ascending a ladder recalls the association commonly established between the rock of the Temple site and the dream of Jacob.[32] It also recalls the concept of the Temple area as the point of access to the Celestial Temple.[33] From these accounts it can be seen that both Ibn al-Faqīh and Ṭabarī viewed the selection of the Temple site as the logical result of its intrinsic importance. Since the importance of the site antedated the Temple, it would also continue after the Temple's destruction.

As can be seen from the accounts cited above Islamic authors generally assumed that David selected the site of the Temple. He was also said by some to have collected materials for its construction and even to have begun the actual building. Muhallabī (d. 990) states that David completed the foundations of the structure.[34]

Although David is often credited with beginning the structure, the vast majority of Islamic accounts of the Temple's construction are related to Solomon's activities. The stories about Solomon and the Temple fall into two groups, those dealing with the actual process of its construction and those which describe its finished appearance. Accounts cited by Ibn al-Faqīh speak of the number of workmen involved in the project, and about the amount of food supplied for their feeding.[35] However, much more popular in the Islamic world were the accounts involving Solomon's use of demonic beings in the Temple's construction. Solomon's ability to control demonic creatures is mentioned in the Qur'ān.[36] One of the tasks executed by them was to build "*miḥrābs*."[37] Although now the word "*miḥrāb*" is used to designate the recess in the wall of a mosque which faces Mekka, the word had originally a more general significance. It appears to have been used to indicate the rooms of honor in dwellings and also to describe buildings containing columns. In the context of the Qur'ān, however, the association of Solomon with the Temple at Jerusalem led to the conclusion that the "*miḥrābs*" were connected with religious structures.[39] Since the term mentioned in the Qur'ān was in the plural it was assumed that the demons had constructed several buildings for Solomon. In various periods Solomon was identified as the builder of religious structures in Alexandria, Yemen and Persepolis.[40] Nevertheless, the "Bayt al-Muqaddas" remained the most important religious structure connected with Solomon.[41]

One of the most popular stories concerning Solomon and the demons describes the manner in which he managed to conceal his death from them by supporting himself on a staff. Only after a worm or termite had gnawed through the staff did he fall, thus revealing to the demons that his control over them had ended. This legend is alluded to in the Qur'ān and given in greater detail by Islamic historians.[42] According to the account in Ṭabarī's history, a number of plants grew spontaneously in the interior of the Temple during its construction. As they grew Solomon removed them and asked each one its use. When one plant replied, "for the destruction of this Temple (*masjid*)" Solomon understood the remark as a prediction of his own death.[43]

Making a staff from this plant Solomon used it to support his body after death, thereby forcing the demons to continue the construction of the Temple. Only after the demons had completed their tasks did the staff break, allowing the demons to regain their freedom.[44] Ṭabarī's version of this story concludes by describing the gratitude of the demons to the termite who had liberated them by destroying the staff of Solomon. As a result demons have been carrying water and clay to the termites ever since.[45]

These anecdotes collected by Ṭabarī were also used by later historians. The *Jāmi' al-Tawārīkh*, "Compendium of Histories," of Rashīd al-Dīn (d. 1318) contains a condensed version of this story. One manuscript of this text was illustrated in the early fifteenth century with a scene showing the construction of the Temple (fig. 26).[46] Solomon stands on the left with his head bowed and leaning on a staff, while the remainder of the painting is filled by a scene showing the demons at work. On the right, one carries a block of stone on his head. Another demon climbs a ladder balancing a heavy load, while a third demon in the center appears to be mixing mortar.

While the stories of Solomon and his deception of the demonic workers captured the popular imagination, legends concerning the decoration of the Temple were of greater significance for the development of Islamic art. The legends concerning Solomon's Temple found in Islamic sources combine legends of pre-Islamic date with interpretations incorporating the Islamic point of view. The description of the Temple found in I Kings 6 and 7 is reflected in some Islamic sources. The most complete use of this tradition occurs in the text of Ibn al-Faqīh who cites as his source Wahb b. Munabbih. Wahb describes the Temple as having stone walls, but with its interior constructed of gilded wood. He also describes the golden doors, the inner shrine and the elaborate decoration of the pair of columns.[47]

Islamic sources contain some more extravagant traditions concerning Solomon's constructions. One of the popular themes is the lavish decoration of his throne. Ṭabarī describes the throne as being of gold inlaid with pearls and jewels.[48] According to Wahb b. Munabbih, as cited by Ibn al-Faqīh, it was the building itself that was encrusted with jewels. He states that Solomon:

> inlaid its ceiling and walls with various rubies and other jewels.[49]

A further development of this theme can be seen in an account by the historian Dīnawarī (d. c. 895), where the gold and jewels are understood to be part of the basic structure of the building.

> It shone in the darkness of a moonless night like a brilliant lamp because of the quantities of jewels and gold used in its construction.[50]

This description would appear to imply that the golden jeweled surfaces were on the outside as well as the inside of the building.

The citation of Wahb ibn Munabbih as the source of this tradition would suggest this legend antedates Islam. Its early assimilation into Islamic traditions is furthermore suggested by its appearance in the history of Dīnawarī. However, the popularity of the association of precious materials with the Temple is not limited to the first centuries of Islam. The same theme appears in an expanded form in a twelfth-century Quranic commentary written in Iran, which concerns the nature of the tasks which the demons performed for Solomon, as mentioned in Sura 34 verse 12. According to this commentary the demons were given the task of collecting precious materials for the Temple. They mined gold, rock, crystal and marble. They collected jewels, amber and musk, and they dove for pearls.[51] Despite these anecdotal details, the result of their labors was to produce a building very similar to that described by Dīnawarī. The Temple was built of white, yellow and green marble. Its columns were made of rock crystal and its roof was constructed of slabs of jewels. The ceilings and walls were inlaid with pearls, emeralds and other jewels, while the floor was paved with sheets of turquoise. When completed, the building "shone in the darkness like the full moon."[52]

With respect to the decoration of the Solomonic Temple, Islamic authors appear to have preferred descriptions which exaggerated its lavishness over the more restrained account offered in the Bible. A similar interest in the fabulous can be seen in the stories concerning the garden of Solomon. In his discussion Ṭabarī mentions trees which grew spontaneously in the Temple during its construction. Solomon would discover the trees when he went to the Temple to pray each morning. Solomon would then inquire of the tree its special properties. After this the tree would be transplanted and information concerning its uses recorded.[53]

This relatively simple account had a more elaborate counterpart. Several related traditions, apparently of Talmudic origin, are recorded by Muhallabī. In his version, the garden consisted of artificial trees made of gold. However, the miraculous nature of the garden was demonstrated by the fact that the artificial trees bore actual fruit.[54]

A further elaboration of this legend is also recorded in Jewish sources, where it is said that the golden trees will lose their fruit if the Temple is desecrated. However, it continues, the trees will bloom again and bear fruit once more when the Temple is rebuilt at the time of the Messiah.[55]

From the information collected above it becomes clear that for the Muslims of the first centuries of Islam, the Solomonic Temple was remembered as one of the key religious monuments of the past. Its construction and destruction mark epochs in man's history. The site of the Temple was the location of miraculous events and the materials used in its construction were the most precious known to man. While most of these legends had their origin in Jewish traditions, the history of the Temple was considered to be part of the past of Islam, since Islam was heir to the biblical tradition. In addition, certain aspects of the legends dealing with the Temple, such as its construction by demons and its opulent decoration, appear to have been further elaborated on by Islamic authors. It should be noted, however, that Islamic sources are far more concerned with the decoration of the Solomonic Temple than with its dimensions or architectural structure.

II

While the attitudes of Muslims toward the Temple of Solomon can be documented in a general manner, it is much more difficult to determine the precise opinion of 'Umar ibn al-Khaṭṭāb about the Temple at the time of his visit to Jerusalem in 17 Hijrah/638 A.D. Jerusalem had capitulated to the Islamic army, but the local citizens had demanded of the regional commander Abū 'Ubaida that the Caliph 'Umar himself come to arrange the terms of the treaty.[56] In addition to arranging the treaty 'Umar appears to have made a visit to the Temple area. After his visit a simple structure was erected to the south of the Rock as a mosque for the local Muslims.[57]

The attitude of 'Umar toward the Temple site is discussed in several accounts of this visit. Although they differ in detail and may well be substantially legendary, the basic implications of the stories are of interest. A major theme in them is the difference between the Muslim and Christian attitudes toward the Temple area.

The simplest account of 'Umar's visit is that of Muhallabī. After speaking of the second destruction of the Temple, he turns to the Christian attitude toward the Temple area. He notes that the Crucifixion and burial of Christ were commemorated by a magnificent church decorated with marble, mosaics and gilded copper. The construction of the church was ordered by Helena, the mother of Constantine. Parallel to the glorification of the area of the city associated with Christ, was the denigration of the Temple area. The abandonment of the Temple site is attributed to Helena:

> She made "the Rock" the garbage dump of the area, and it passed into oblivion.[58]

By way of contrast, Muhallabī credits 'Umar with a partial revival of the Temple area. After the conquest the Jews showed 'Umar the Temple site and 'Umar ordered it to be cleaned. The Muslims and Jews cooperated in this task, after which the Muslims built a sanctuary in the area.[59] Thus, in the account of Muhallabī, 'Umar appears to understand the significance of the Temple area.

More elaborate accounts of 'Umar's visit appear in Ṭabarī's history. The simpler version is attributed to Abū Maryam, the client of Salāma, who claims to have been an eyewitness to the visit. 'Umar went to "al-Masjid," by which Abū Maryam appears to mean the site of the former Temple, and then proceeded to the "Miḥrāb of David."

> he entered it and recited "the Prayer of David," then he prayed and we prayed with him.[50]

Although this reference is not precise, it would suggest that the "Miḥrāb of David" was located near the site of the former Temple. The "Prayer of David" refers to several verses in the 38th Sura describing the manner in which David was tempted by divine messengers into giving a hasty and erroneous judgment in a dispute over sheep.[61] Realizing his mistake David asks God's forgiveness, which is granted with a warning:

> Oh David, we made you a deputy (*khalīfa*) on earth
> So you might judge between people justly.[62]

The "Prayer of David," therefore, relates not to the building of the Temple but to the responsibilities of rulers to execute God's laws with justice, and their need for repentance whenever those laws are violated. Since the Qur'ān specifies that the incident occurred in "the miḥrāb," the setting of the event became known as "the Miḥrāb of David."[63]

The theme of 'Umar's respect for the Temple area is emphasized in the second version of this incident given by Ṭabarī. It, too, is said to derive from an eyewitness account, although related on the authority of Rajā' ibn Ḥaywah, a leading theologian at the courts of the 'Umayyad rulers 'Abd al-Malik, Walīd, Sulaymān, and 'Umar II.[64] In this account 'Umar addresses God as he enters the "Masjid:"

> Here I stand before you God in a place which is dearest to you.[65]

When he goes to the "Miḥrāb of David" and begins to pray, night is transformed into day. Then the Muezzin is ordered to call the Muslim community to prayer. 'Umar prays with them and recites for them the 38th Sura which contains the "Prayer of David" as well as references to Solomon, Job and other Prophets. As his second recitation 'Umar chooses the first verse of Sura 17 which describes the "Night Journey" or "Isrā' " of the Prophet Muḥammad.[66] The inclusion of this reference suggests that for the author of this tradition the goal of the Prophet's nocturnal voyage was the Temple area in Jerusalem.

The second section of the passage in Ṭabarī deals with the relationship between the Islamic, Jewish and Christian attitudes toward "the Rock" in the center of Mt. Moriah. 'Umar represents the Muslim viewpoint, while the remarks attributed to Ka'b ibn al-Aḥbar, a Jewish convert to Islam, are both pro-Jewish and anti-Christian. Although this account is essentially a theological debate it is presented in a manner at once colloquial and highly dramatic. The remarks of 'Umar are brusque while those of Ka'b contain complex allusions and prophecies.

Following the completion of his prayers 'Umar orders Ka'b to be brought before him. Ka'b advises 'Umar to construct a Muslim place of worship (*muṣallā*) "on the Rock." 'Umar rejects this idea as representing "Jewishness," stating that it is the Kaaba in Mekka and not the Rock in Jerusalem which must be used by Muslims as the direction of prayer. 'Umar then goes to "the garbage dump under which the *Rūm* had buried Bayt al-Muqaddas."[67] When 'Umar bends down to collect the garbage in the skirt of his garment,

Ka'b exclaims "Allāh Akbar" (God is great). 'Umar, irritated at this seeming irreverence, interrogates Ka'b once more. As a justification for his reaction Ka'b claims "a Prophet prophesied five hundred years ago about what you did today," the prophecy being:

> Rejoice, oh Jerusalem, for there will be the Fārūq (i.e. 'Umar) who will cleanse you from what is upon you.[68]

While this part of the account appears to be implicitly anti-Christian, attributing the desecration of the temple to the "Rūm" a name which usually refers to the Byzantines; the second "prophecy" is overtly hostile to the Christians, threatening the destruction of Constantinople in retaliation for their attitude toward the Temple.

> Oh, Constantinople, what did your people do to my house? They destroyed it . . . so I have passed Judgment over you: I shall make you bare, and no one will seek refuge in you.[69]

This prophesy clearly has little to do with 'Umar's visit or the location of a Muslim place of worship. It appears to be related to the body of legends which enveloped the attempts of Muslim armies to capture Constantinople. The mention of refuge suggests that the text refers to the siege of Constantinople led by Yazīd b. Mu'āwiya in 48-49/668-669. Muslim traditions speak of Yazīd's forcing the Byzantine army to take refuge within the city walls, although Byzantine sources contain no references to such an incident.[70] It is thus possible that the dramatic version of 'Umar's visit transmitted by Rajā' ibn Ḥaywah was created to provide a theological rationale for the assault on Constantinople which occurred during the reign of the Caliph Sulaymān, 97-99/715-717. This assault, led by the Caliph's brother Maslama b. 'Abd al-Malik, was to end in failure, but Muslim legends assert that Maslama managed not only to enter the city but to desecrate the church of Hagia Sophia.[71]

Although it is not certain that this tradition relates to the propaganda circulated concerning the 'Ummayad ruler Sulaymān, the implication given is that the fall of Constantinople is the punishment due the Christians for their destruction of the Temple.[72] This tradition demonstrates the manner in which the antagonism between the 'Ummayads and Byzantines led the Muslim rulers to adopt positions in harmony with those of the Jewish community. Al-Bīrūnī relates another tradition about 'Umar with a similar flavor. When 'Umar arrived in Syria, the Jews of Damascus came to him urging the capture of Jerusalem. They said: "You are the Lord of Aelia," i.e. Jerusalem, implying that the Islamic conquest of that city had been foretold.[73]

While it is probably impossible to reconstruct the attitude of 'Umar himself toward the site of the Temple, complex symbolic interpretations of his actions appear to have been in circulation by the early eighth century. All of these traditions imply a respect for and knowledge of the area's past history. However, the connections between the actions of 'Umar and those of 'Abd al-Malik and Walīd have not yet been established. According to an inscription and historical references, 'Abd al-Malik ordered the construction of the Dome of the Rock around "the Rock" on Mt. Moriah (fig. 27). This project was apparently completed in 72 Hijra/691-692.[74] Documents and some archaeological evidence make it likely that Walīd was responsible for constructing a congregational Mosque on the site of the present al-Aqṣā Mosque, that is to the south of the Dome of the Rock. This is also probably the general vicinity of the "Muṣallā" erected on the orders of 'Umar discussed above.[75]

It has been suggested that 'Abd al-Malik's purpose in building the Dome of the Rock was to symbolize "the superiority and victory of Islam" over its Byzantine and Sasanian opponents. The victory over these powers is thought to be expressed in the use of jeweled crowns in the mosaic decoration of the structure (fig. 30).[76] In addition, a clear anti-Christological theme is discernible in the Quranic quotations used in the building.[77] On the other hand, Walīd's construction of a congregational mosque on the southern part of the Temple area has been connected with the recognition of Jerusalem as the goal of the Prophet's "Night Journey."[78]

While the relationship of religious and political concepts in the 'Umayyad period appears to have been quite complex, the literary evidence suggests that the primary associations with Jerusalem were religious. Although the chronology of the development of the Islamic attitude toward Jerusalem is a complex problem, the textual evidence suggests a slow yet consistent accumulation of traditions around the central concept of the recognition of the sanctity of the area. The connection of the Prophet's "Night Journey" with the Temple area can be seen as the logical conclusion of this development.[79]

It would thus seem possible to view the actions of 'Abd al-Malik in constructing the Dome of the Rock as an expression of respect for the religious associations of the site. This would then create a progression from 'Umar to 'Abd al-Malik to Walīd, in which their actions would represent an increasing "Islamization" of the sacred area. Their activities would, however, be based on a recognition of the past associations with the Temple area.

With respect to the Dome of the Rock, its inscriptions, as has been established, clearly refer to aspects of Christianity rejected by Islam; the Virgin Birth, the Incarnation, and the Trinity. This theme would appear to be an elaboration of the antagonism toward the Christian shrines commemorating the Crucifixion and Resurrection seen in the legends concerning 'Umar's visit.

By way of contrast the principal link between the Dome of the Rock as constructed by 'Abd al-Malik and the tradition of the Solomonic Temple appears to be the mosaic decoration of the building's interior. While there is no description of the decorative scheme of the Dome of the Rock in Islamic sources, which would make this connection explicit, there are certain parallels between the literary traditions connected with Solomon's Temple and the decoration of the Islamic structure.[80]

The building is composed of an octagonal external wall

with four entrances oriented to the points of the compass and two zones of columns and piers which support the roof. The outer zone is octagonal while the inner one around the Rock itself is circular.[81] The best preserved and most significant mosaic decoration is located on the arches and piers of the octagonal zone.

The outer surface of the octagonal zone is decorated with trees having multi-colored trunks, luxuriant blossoms and clusters of fruit, predominantly grapes.[82] Trees also appear on the inner side of the octagonal arcade where they are located on the short side of the piers (fig. 28).[83] Some of the trees appear quite naturalistic but others have trunks inlaid with jewels.[84] A third type of "tree" appearing on the piers bears naturalistic fruit, but is constructed of plant forms growing out of jeweled bases and bearing collars of jewels and gold (fig. 29).[85]

It would seem reasonable to connect these unusual trees and tree-like forms with the golden trees associated with Solomon's Temple. The realistic depiction of certain details, particularly the fruit, combined with the imaginary character of the whole scheme accords well with the traditions recorded by Muhallabī of golden trees bearing real fruit.[86] While the date of Muhallabī's geographical treatise precludes its being used as testimony on the attitudes of the time of 'Abd al-Malik, the traditions which he cites were already mentioned in the Babylonian Talmud.[87] This suggests that the legends of Solomon's golden garden could have passed into Islamic sources at a date considerably prior to its use by Muhallabī.

The central surface of the piers on the inner side of the octagonal zone is decorated with a pair of vine-like plants rising from acanthus leaves.[88] While some of the plants appear to be naturalistic in certain details, their stems are often incrusted with jewels and crowns, and are suspended between the two vines (fig. 30).[89] The combination of jewels and plants continues on the arches of this zone. The plants rise from jeweled pedestal-like bases and are laden with golden crowns and ornaments which are inlaid with simulated jewels and pearls.[90] Only at its furthest extension does the plant resume its vegetal character bearing both blossoms and fruit. In all sections of the decoration of this zone there is an abundant use of mother of pearl chips along with mosaic cubes.[91]

This use of jeweled decoration recalls the tradition cited by Wahb ibn Munabbih and Dīnawarī that the walls and ceiling of the Temple were inlaid with jewels. The luminosity created by the golden mosaics, and mother of pearl chips also coincides with the brilliance ascribed to the decoration of the Solomonic Temple in these same texts.[92] While the date and origin of these traditions concerning the luminous jeweled decoration of the Solomonic Temple have not yet been established, their attribution to Wahb ibn Munabbih suggests that they were known in the 'Umayyad period. While it is obvious that the Dome of the Rock is not an attempt to recreate the Solomonic Temple in its totality, the character of its decoration suggests that the memory of the magnificent decoration of the earlier structure was influential in the selection of decorative themes for the Islamic building.

In addition to the theme of golden trees and jeweled ornaments, the building's decoration contains numerous allusions to earthly abundance. The trees and vines are often laden with various types of fruit, of which grapes and dates appear to predominate. The most direct allusion to abundance appears to be on the arch soffits of the octagonal zone.[93] Some of them have grape vines heavily laden with grapes.[94] Others are covered with garlands of fruit or various types of cornucopias.[95] Among the fruits identified in addition to grapes and dates are figs, pears, apples, prunes, quince, pomegranates, olives, cherries and citron.[96]

It is tempting to connect these decorative evocations of abundance with the Quranic phrases about "the land which we have blessed" often associated with Jerusalem. While the theme of the fertility of Jerusalem is not given prominence by Islamic historians the idea is referred to by al-Muqaddasī (d. c. 991), a geographer born in Jerusalem. In a passage describing the extent of the territory of Jerusalem he comments "this is the Blessed Land spoken of by God the Almightly," an apparent reference to Quranic passages such as Sura 21 verses 71 and 81 discussed above. As manifestations of this blessedness he cites the growing of crops without artificial irrigation or rivers, which he interprets as related to the "Promised Land" which is "flowing with milk and honey."[97] Another manifestation of Jerusalem's abundance is the presence in it of many types of fruit normally associated with diverse climates:

> Such mutually exclusive things as citron, almonds, dates, walnuts, figs and bananas.[98]

Thus the image of an earthly paradise with an abundance of fruit of many types, suggested by the decoration of the Dome of the Rock, finds its counterpart in traditions associated with the area in Islamic times.

III

While the construction of the Dome of the Rock on a site already sanctified by earlier religious practice appears to be suitable for a religion which considers itself to be the inheritor of earlier traditions, the role of the Temple site in the stories of the Prophet Muhammad's "Night Journey" and "Ascension" is more difficult to evaluate. The focal point of discussions on this subject was the text of the initial verse of Sura 17:

> Praise to Him who made His Servant travel by night from the Masjid al-Ḥarām to the Masjid al-Aqṣā.

The identification of Masjid al-Ḥarām with the sanctuary of the Kaaba in Mekka was easily made, but the identity of "al-Masjid al-Aqṣā," the Furthermost Sanctuary, was the subject of debate among Muslims as it has been among modern scholars of Islam.[99] One tradition known to the local historians of Mekka connects this term with a small sanctuary on the outskirts of Mekka itself.[100] A second opinion identified Masjid al-Aqṣā as being in Heaven.[101] The third interpretation connected Masjid al-Aqṣā with Jerusalem and particularly with the site of the former Temple. Although the origin and growth of this concept is obscure it would appear to have been gaining support by the early eighth century at about the time when Walīd began construction of a Congregational Mosque in Jerusalem.[102]

Underlying the connection of Masjid al-Aqṣā with the Temple area would appear to be the various traditions concerning the inherent sanctity of the location rather than its particular connection with Solomon's Temple. Some Islamic religious scholars asserted that all prophets were either from the Palestinian region or were transported there in a Night Visit.[103] Since it was clear that many of these ideas were closely paralleled by rabbinic traditions, the enthusiasm for Jerusalem as the home of prophets was by no means universal among Muslim theologians.[104]

However, as the interpretations of the first verse of Sura 17 grew in complexity Jerusalem was regarded as the goal of the Prophet's "Night Journey" and the place from which he ascended to Heaven.[105] The explanation for the association of the "Ascension to Heaven" with Jerusalem would appear to be the notion that Jerusalem was located directly below the "Celestial Temple," another rabbinic tradition which had a wide circulation in the early centuries of Islam.[106]

The role of the Temple site in these legends can be seen from an account of the Prophet's "Night Journey" attributed to Ḥasan al-Baṣrī (d. 728) and contained in the biography of the Prophet written by Ibn Isḥāq (d.c.768). Jerusalem is mentioned in connection with three different episodes. Upon his arrival in Jerusalem the Prophet Muhammad is greeted by Abraham, Moses and Jesus, and a number of other prophets, who ask him to lead them in communal prayer. This ceremony takes place in "Bayt al-Muqaddas." Immediately after the prayer the Prophet is presented with bowls of wine and milk. He chooses to drink the milk leaving the wine, a decision applauded by his guide the angel Gabriel.[107] While the incident of Muhammad as *Imām* for the other prophets implies their recognition of his superior position, the choice of milk appears to provide divine sanction for the Islamic prohibition against the consumption of wine. Although Jerusalem would seem a suitable location for the encounter involving prophets, its connection with the prohibition of wine is obscure.

While in some versions of the legend the prayer of the Prophets is merely a prelude to Muhammad's journey through Heaven and Hell, in the version of Ḥasan al-Baṣrī he returns immediately to Mekka. The next morning he tells the citizens of Mekka about his miraculous voyage. This story is greeted with incredulity and even hostility. The Quraysh, the local aristocracy, are particularly vocal in their disbelief. In order to verify that he has indeed been to Jerusalem he is asked to describe it to Abū Bakr, one of his most loyal followers. Abū Bakr, who apparently had some previous knowledge of the city, certifies that the Prophet's description is correct.[108]

Since the association of the site of the former Temple with the "Night Journey" of the Prophet created an interpretation of the site which for Islam overshadowed all previous traditions, it is appropriate to conclude this discussion of Solomon's Temple with three paintings which show the Temple site and the Prophet.

The first, taken from a fifteenth-century manuscript copied and illustrated in Herat, shows the Prophet Muhammad leading the other prophets in prayer (fig. 31).[109] The Prophet is shown in the center of the painting with a flaming halo, seated on a carpet. Since the wall behind him appears to contain a prayer-niche in which a lamp is suspended, the building in which the prophets are meeting would appear to be a mosque. The text identifies the setting as "Bayt al-Muqaddas," a term used for both the Temple and the surrounding city.[110]

When asked to depict the setting of the Prophet's visit to Jerusalem, artists were presented with a perplexing problem. Actually during his lifetime the site must have been covered with refuse and devoid of any buildings. The various interpretations given to the term "Masjid al-Aqṣā" would appear to be related to the ambiguous state of the Temple area in the first years of the Islamic period. One possible solution is that followed by Muqaddasī, who uses the term as equivalent to the whole Temple site.[111] Another solution was to equate the site of the visit with the mosque located on the southern section of the platform on Mt. Moriah which was begun by Walīd and rebuilt by later rulers.[112] This may be the solution used by the painter of the manuscript now in Paris.

There was, however, a third possibility which was used by the painter of a more complex rendition of the Prophet's visit (fig. 32).[113] In this painting of the middle fourteenth century the building appears to be constructed in the proximity of "the Rock," since that feature is given clearly in the foreground of the painting. The upper section shows a building constructed with a polygonal arcade composed of pairs of columns. The columns and the niche behind Muhammad have the appearance of marble. The rear wall of the building is apparently gilded and decorated with engraved arabesque scrolls.

Two interpretations of this structure can be suggested. One is that it represents the Dome of the Rock as it was known to a painter in Iran. The other possibility is that it represents an imaginary structure combining features from Solomon's Temple, as it was described in Islamic texts, with some aspects of the Dome of the Rock.[114]

While the identification of the Solomonic Temple as "Masjid al-Aqṣā" would appear an historical impossibility, it is found in some texts. In his geographical treatise the Iranian scholar Ḥamd Allāh Mustawfī (d.c.1340) describes the building begun by David and completed by Solomon as "Masjid al-Aqṣā."[115] A more elaborate example of the merger of the two traditions is found in the poetry of Jalāl al-

Dīn Rūmī (d. 1273). His description of the construction of Solomon's Temple is announced as "the story of the construction of Masjid al-Aqṣā." The description itself includes references to the stone walls and decoration of the building. He mentions "light glistening from mother of pearl chips" and the presence of trees and fruit. The structure is compared to "Paradise."[116] All of these images suggest that he was combining the physical features of the Dome of the Rock with traditions associated with Solomon's Temple in a manner analagous to that used by the painter of the Prophet's visit.

While it appears possible that the setting of the event is "Masjid al-Aqṣā," imagined as a structure resembling both the Dome of the Rock and the Solomonic Temple, the explanation for other aspects of the painting is more complex. The main event is clearly the presentation to Muhammad of the bowls containing various liquids, of which he will choose milk. This presentation is being witnessed by another figure seated next to Muhammad and closely resembling him in dress and facial features. While the similar dress suggests that this person is also a Prophet, the resemblance of his facial type to that of Muhammad suggests his identity. Of all the Prophets the one said to be most like Muhammad was Abraham. At times they are said to have a virtually identical appearance.[117]

The identity of the other figures, many of whom appear to be ignoring the Prophets and the angels, is more obscure. Since similar figures appear in the third painting to be discussed a tentative identification of their significance will be made following the discussion of that work.

The third painting would appear to be by the same artist who painted the scene of the Prophet choosing milk in the Masjid al-Aqṣā.[118] This painting shows the Prophet seated on a carpet conversing with two men who kneel before him. Another group of spectators, some of whom resemble figures seen in the previous illustration, face the Prophet and his companions. Most of these people appear to be talking among themselves, and two other figures stand on the right facing away from Muhammad. Two features suggest the presence of supernatural forces. The Prophet is shown surrounded by a flaming golden halo; an angel hovers unnoticed over the Prophet's companions, carrying a walled city (fig. 33).

Although no text accompanies this painting, it would appear to represent the vision of Jerusalem granted to Muhammad during his attempts to convince the citizens of Mekka that he had indeed visited the "Masjid al-Aqṣā." The connection of a vision with the Prophet's "Night Journey" can be seen in the interpretations given to the 60th verse of Sura 17:

> We created the Vision which you saw as a test for the people.

According to the remarks collected by Ṭabarī, the early authorities equated the "vision" with the whole experience of the Prophet in his journey. All that he saw was a "vision," not a dream.[119] There were, however, dissenters to this point of view; some felt that the "vision" was in fact a dream, while others felt that the "vision" was granted to him in Mekka after his return from the journey.[120]

The intepretation of the "vision" as a dream would appear to be in harmony with the interpretation of the whole experience of the "Night Journey" as a spiritual rather than a physical voyage. This interpretation was favored by 'Ā'isha, the Prophet's wife, and Mu'āwiyah, the first Caliph of the 'Umayyad house.[121]

There was, however, another interpretation of the Prophet's "vision" which was connected with the hostile reaction of the Quraysh to the story of his journey. While the hostile reaction of the citizens of Mekka to the Prophet's recounting of his voyage is mentioned by many authorities, one legend gives the Prophet's encounter with the Quaraysh a more dramatic quality. According to this tradition, cited by Ṭabarī, when the Quraysh refused to believe the Prophet's story of his journey, God showed him "Bayt al-Muqaddas," which Muhammad was then able to describe to them.[122]

The various traditions regarding the Prophet's miraculous journey were woven together in a continuous narrative in later periods. Although the exact process of development is not yet known, the painting in Istanbul shows a much more complex story than that found in Ṭabarī's citation of isolated traditions. Although the text which originally accompanied the paintings is lost, the version of the event found in an unpublished Persian *Mi'rāj-*

Nāmeh provides useful parallels.[123] This text gives a direct and vivid, if somewhat simplified, description of the Prophet's reactions to this miraculous voyage.

After the voyage the Prophet returned to the house of 'Umm Hānī', the daughter of his uncle Abū Ṭālib. When 'Umm Hānī' hears his story, she is incredulous and tries to prevent him from going to "the Mosque" to tell others about his voyage. While in the mosque the Prophet, in the presence of Abū Ṭālib and various Mekkan citizens, repeats his story once more. One member of the group, Mʻufī ibn ʻAdā, jumps to his feet in anger and accuses the Prophet of lying.[124] At this point Abū Bakr is persuaded to join the group to listen to the Prophet's story. After repeating once more the chief features of his voyage, the Prophet is asked by Abū Bakr to describe the "Masjid Bayt al-Muqaddas." When the Prophet obliges, Abū Bakr verifies the description as correct. The incident is terminated by Abū Bakr's recitation of the Quranic verses describing the Prophet's "Night Journey" and his Vision (Sura 17, verses 1 and 60).[125]

By taking the details of this story and combining them with the traditions cited above, it is possible to make a tentative identification of all the groups in the painting. Facing the Prophet are Abū Ṭālib and Abū Bakr. Judging by the gestures of the Prophet and Abū Bakr, it is the moment when the Prophet is describing "Masjid al-Aqṣā" to him. The spectators, probably the Quraysh, show varied reactions to the event. Two of them have obviously, like Mʻufī ibn ʻAdā, decided to reject the Prophet's explanation.

Judging by their similarity with the spectators in this scene, those shown in the painting of the Prophet's choice of milk must also be the citizens of Mekka (figs. 32-33). Their exact role is somewhat obscure, but the painting may in fact represent the Prophet's voyage to Jerusalem as a spiritual experience of which he alone was aware. Thus even those gathered around him were unaware of its occurrence.

Although the gestures of the main groups of figures in the scene of the Prophet's vision fit into the narrative found in other sources, the city-scape held by the angel must still be explained. Some sources speak of the Prophet's vision of Masjid al-Aqṣā as providing him with the details necessary to give an accurate account of the site during his argument with the Quraysh, who disputed his claim to have traveled to Jerusalem and back in one night.[126] It would thus seem likely that the structures shown are connected with "Masjid al-Aqṣā" or "Masjid Bayt al-Muqaddas." Since another painting by this same artist would appear to connect the Dome of the Rock with "Masjid al-Aqṣā," a modified version of that structure should be present. While the details are somewhat difficult to analyze, the center of the scene held by the angel would appear to contain a small round building surrounded by a wall. In front of the round structure is a rectangular building. It is possible that these two buildings represent the Dome of the Rock and the Congregational Mosque in the Temple area.

Although these small structures have certain similarities with the Islamic monuments of the Temple area, the presence of rivers in the city-scape would appear to preclude its identification with Jerusalem. Geographical descriptions of Jerusalem emphasize the aridity of the city. Lacking a spring, the water supply was limited to rain water gathered in cisterns. Not only were the houses all equipped with cisterns, but even the water falling into the city streets was carefully stored for later use.[127]

However, the natural geographical conditions of Jerusalem were apparently less significant to this painter than the religious traditions concerning the presence of a spring under "the Rock" of Bayt al-Muqaddas.[128] In more elaborate versions of this tradition the Tigris, the Euphrates, the Nile and the Oxus are all said to be derived from this miraculous source.[129] Thus the presence of the rivers in the city-scape held by the angel is one further indication that the artist's intention was to portray "Masjid al-Aqṣā" as "Bayt al-Muqaddas."

With these paintings the process of the "Islamization" of the Temple area has been completed. Not only has the association of the Prophet's "Night Journey" become the most significant manifestation of the sanctity of the area, but even the Solomonic Temple has been absorbed into the Islamic heritage. Thus the attributes of the Dome of the Rock were merged with the memories of the Solomonic structure not only by Jalāl al-Dīn Rūmī in his poetic description, but by the painter of the early fourteenth-century al-Bīrūnī manuscript. The resemblance noted above between the Solomonic Temple destroyed by Bukhtnaṣṣar (fig. 25) and the Dome of the Rock appears to be part of a larger tendency to merge the two traditions.

Although the exact chronology of all aspects of the problem has not been established, the Islamic attitude toward the Solomonic Temple appears to have three main elements which were given varying prominence in different periods of Islamic history. First, there is a basic acceptance of the historical and religious importance of the Temple site and of the building itself. This point of view is implicit in Quranic passages, and was made explicit by traditions used in Quranic commentary. Paradoxically, however, the associations of holiness were more clearly attached to the site than to the Solomonic Temple itself. The Temple building proper was remembered for its opulent and even magical decoration with jewels and golden trees.

Secondly, the Christian attitude toward the Temple area is clearly attacked. That the construction of buildings in the vicinity of the former Temple should be viewed as an attempt to de-emphasize the Christian sanctuaries appears clear from the inscriptional and historical evidence. It should, however, be noted that the anti-Christian statements in historians such as Ṭabarī are interwoven with the history of the conflicts between the Muslim and Christian armies during the 'Umayyad period. Thus the anti-Christian aspects of the Islamic attitude toward the Temple region were destined to recede in importance as the Muslim community turned its attention to other matters.

The third and final element was to integrate the aura of

sanctity surrounding the Temple area with the religious experience of the Prophet Muhammad. The growth of this theme is very difficult to trace in part because it represents an extension and modification of attitudes implicit in the attitude toward the Temple site mentioned above. To use Jerusalem as the site of the Prophet's encounters with the earlier Prophets and as the point of departure for his visit to Heaven and Hell was to insure that Jerusalem would retain its status as one of the most hallowed places on earth. However, the integration of the Temple area in the legends surrounding the Prophet's "Night Journey" served to glorify the site, not the Solomonic Temple. Solomon is not among the religious figures who pray with Muhammad in "Masjid Bayt al-Muqaddas."

In conclusion it can be suggested that the actions of 'Abd al-Malik, and probably 'Umar in constructing buildings in the Temple area reflects a combination of the first and second themes—a partial continuation of traditions of the Solomonic Temple combined with a rejection of Christian ideas. The exact moment when these attitudes were replaced with the identification of Bayt al-Muqaddas as "Masjid al-Aqṣā" is very difficult to establish. The triumph of this association must be linked with a decline in the importance of the Temple area in anti-Christian propaganda as well as with the growth of pietistic legends within the Islamic community.

1. Concerning the mosque constructed by 'Umar b. al-Khaṭṭāb see K. A. C. Creswell, *Early Muslim Architecture* I (Oxford, 1969), 29-35. (Hereafter E.M.A.)

2. Concerning the Dome of the Rock see Creswell, *op. cit.*, 65-131 and 213-322, and also O. Grabar, "The Umayyad Dome of the Rock in Jerusalem," *Ars Orientalis* 3 (1959), 33-62.

3. Concerning the "Night Journey" see B. Schrieke, "Isrā' " *Encyclopedia of Islam*, 1st ed. (hereafter E.I.[1]); for the "Ascension" see J. Horovitz, "Mi'rādj," E.I.[1]

4. 'Alī b. al-Husayn known as al-Mas'ūdī, *Murūj al-Dhahab* ed. Pavet de Courteille, Barbier de Meynard, IV (Paris, 1914), 56-57. *Murūj al-Dhahab* was apparently completed in 947 and revised in 956. For biographical information see C. Brockelmann, "Mas'ūdī" E.I.[1]

5. 'Abd Allāh b. Muslim known as Ibn Qutayba, *Kitāb al-Ma'ārif* (Cairo, 1969), 32 lines 2-3. For biographical data see G. Lecomte, "Ibn Ḳutayba, *Encyclopedia of Islam*, 2nd ed. (Hereafter E.I.[2])

6. On the role of Wahb ibn Munabbih see F. Rosenthal, "The Influence of the Biblical Tradition on Muslim Historiography," in *Historians of the Middle East*, ed. B. Lewis and P. M. Holt (London, 1962), 40-45, and A. Guillaume, *The Life of Muhammad* (Oxford, 1955), XV.

7. Hamza Isfahānī, *Ta'rikh sānī mulūk al-arḍ wa al-anbiyā'*, al-Hayat (Beirut, n.d.), 77-78. For more information see F. Rosenthal, "Hamza Isfahānī," E.I.[2]

8. Abū Rayḥān Muḥammad al-Bīrūnī, *al-Āthār al-bāqīya 'an al-qurūn al-khālīya*, ed. E. Sachau (Leipzig, 1923), 17-19, and al-Bīrūnī, *The Chronology of Ancient Nations*, trans. E. Sachau, (London, 1879), 20-22.

9. al-Bīrūnī, *Āthār*, 36-37; *Chronology*, 43-44.

10. Hamza Isfahānī, *Ta'rīkh*, 78.

11. al-Bīrūnī, *Āthār*, 282; *Chronology*, 276.

12. Edinburgh University Library, Arab 161, fol. 158v. The manuscript is dated to 707 Hijrah/1307-08. Published by B. Gray, *Persian Painting* (Geneva, 1961), 27.

13. al-Bīrūnī, *Āthār*, 282:16-17; for the history and use of the various names for Jerusalem, see F. Buhl, "al-Ḳuds" E.I.[1]

14. Qur'ān, Sura 17, verse 7.

15. Muḥammad b. Jarīr known as al-Ṭabarī, *Jāmi' al-Bayān* XV (Cairo, 1954), 43.

16. *Ibid.*, 34-35.

17. *Ibid.*, 33, 35.

18. *Ibid.*, 31-43 for "Bayt al- Muqaddas," 43 for "Masjid Bayt al-Muqaddas."

19. Ahmad ibn Yaḥyā known as al-Balādhurī, *Kitāb Futūḥ al-Buldān*, ed. M. J. de Goeje (Leiden, 1968), 15.

20. "The Holy Land": Sura 5, verse 20; "The Land which we have Blessed" Sura 21, verses 71, and 81. See also, S. D. Goitein, "The Sanctity of Jerusalem and Palestine in Early Islam," in *Studies in Islamic History and Institutions* (Leiden, 1966), especially 143-147.

21. For example see Ibn al-Faqīh, *Kitāb al- Buldān*, ed. M. J. de Goeje (Leiden, 1885), 99: 14-16.

22. M. J. Kister, "You shall only set out for three Mosques: A Study of an Early Tradition," *Le Museon* 82 (1969), 173-196, esp. 182-187.

23. For "the Holy Land" see Ṭabarī, *Jāmi' al-Bayān*, VI, 171-172. For Sura 21, verse 71, see *ibid.*, VI, 46-47.

24. *Ibid.*, 46.
25. *Ibid.*, 46-47.
26. Ibn al-Faqīh, *Kitāb al-Buldān*, 93-102.
27. *Ibid.*, 93: 13-15.
28. *Ibid.*, 93-94.
29. *Ibid.*, 98: 5-16.
30. Muḥammad b. Jarīr, known as al-Ṭabarī, *Ta'rīkh al-Rusul wa 'l-Mulūk*, I/2, 571-75.
31. *Ibid.*, 571: 8- 572:7.
32. For example in the text of Ibn Qutayba who cites Wahb ibn Munabbih as his authority, *Kitāb al-Ma'ārif*, 39.
33. J. W. Hirschberg, "The Sources of Moslem Traditions concerning Jerusalem," in *Rocznik Orientalistyczny* 17 (1951-52), 321-322; 325, 327.
34. Ḥasan b. Aḥmad al-Muhallabī, *Kitāb al-Masālik wa 'l-mamālik*, published by Ṣalāḥ al-Dīn Munajjid, "Qit'ah min kitāb mafqūd al-masālik wa al-mamālik li'l-Muhallabī," *Majallah Ma'had al-Makhṭūṭāt al-'Arabīyah* IV (Cairo, 1958), 52; for mention of David's work see also Aḥmad b. Dā'ūd al-Dīnawarī, *al-Akhbār al-Ṭiwāl* (Cairo, 1960), 21:3. 21:3.
35. Ibn al-Faqīh, *Kitāb al- Buldān*, 96:1-3; 98:19-22.
36. Qur'ān, Sura 21, verse 81.
37. *Ibid.*, Sura 34, verse 12.
38. R. B. Sergeant, "Miḥrāb," *Bulletin of the School of Oriental and African Studies* 22 (1959), 439-453.

39. Ṭabarī, *Jāmi' al-Bayān* XXII, 70, where *"masājid,"* sanctuaries, is the most frequently cited synonym for *"maḥārīb"* although other equivalents such as *"quṣūr"* = fortifications, and *"masākin"* = dwellings are also mentioned. In his history, Ṭabarī mentions a *"miḥrāb"* as the part of "Bayt al-Muqaddas" where Solomon prays. (*Ta'rīkh*, I/2, 595:15-596:7).

40. In Alexandria according to Ḥamd Allāh Mustawfī, *The Geographical Part of Nuzhat al-Qulūb*, ed. G. Le Strange (Leiden, 1915-1919), 248; in Yemen according to 'Alī b. Abū Bakr al-Harawī, *Kitāb al-Ishārāt 'ilā Ma'rifat al-Ziyārāt*, ed. J. Sourdel-Thomine (Damascus, 1953), 97; in Persepolis by many authors including Mas'ūdī, *Murūj al-Dhahab*, IV, 76-77.

41. For example, in Bal'amī's adaptation of Ṭabarī's history, the Jerusalem Temple is the only building mentioned by name. Muhammad Bal'amī, *Chronique*, trans. H. Zotenberg I (Paris, 1958), 434-435.

42. The Qur'ān, Sura 34, verse 13 speaks of a worm, but Ṭabarī refers to a termite, *Ta'rīkh*, I/2, 597, line 2.

43. Ṭabarī, *Ta'rīkh*, I/2, 594-595, esp. 594:15-16, 595:15.

44. *Ibid.*, 595-596.

45. *Ibid.*, 597:1-6. A condensed version of these episodes is also found in Bal'amī (*Chronique* I, 454-456.)

46. Rashīd al-Dīn, *Jāmi' al-Tawārīkh*, Istanbul, Topkapî Sarayî Müzesi Kütüphanesi, Hazine 1654, fol. 18v.

47. Ibn al-Faqīh, *Kitāb al-Buldān*, 98:22-99:9.

48. Ṭabari, *Ta'rīkh* I/2, 584:6-10.

49. Ibn al- Faqīh, *Kitāb al-Buldān*, 99:10-11.

50. Dīnawarī, *Akhbār al-Ṭiwāl*, 21:5-6.

51. Abū 'Alī al-Faḍl al-Tabarsī, *Majma' al-Bayān* XXII (Cairo, 1955), 191.

52. *Ibid.*

53. Ṭabarī, *Ta'rīkh* I/2, 595:8-13. The source is given as "companions of the Prophet" transmitted by Ibn Mas'ūd; a shorter version is attributed to the Prophet himself, *ibid.*, 594.

54. Muhallabī, *al-Masālik wa al-Mamālik*, ed. Munajjid, 52; also G. Vajda, "La description du Temple de Jérusalem d'après le K. al-masālik wal-mamālik d'al-Muhallabī: ses éléments bibliques et rabbiniques," *Journal Asiatique* 247 (1959), 195-196.

55. L. Ginzberg, The Legends of the Jews IV (Philadelphia, 1913), 154.

56. al-Balādhurī, *Futūḥ al-Buldān*, 138-139.

57. Creswell, E.M.A.² vol. I/1, 32-35.

58. Muhallabī, *al-Masālik wa al-Mamālik*, 53-54, quotation from 54. The building in question is the Church of the Holy Sepulchre begun under Constantine and rebuilt in later periods. For further information see R. Krautheimer, *Early Christian and Byzantine Architecture* (Baltimore, 1965), 39-41. In Islamic texts this church is called "al-Qiyāma," the Resurrection, or "al-Qamāma" the Dungheap. Muhallabī does not give its name.

59. Muhallabī, *al-Masālik wa al-Mamālik*, 54.

60. Ṭabarī, *Ta'rīkh* I/6, 2408, lines 5-8.

61. The incident is recounted in Sura 38, verses 20-25.

62. *Ibid.*, Sura 38, verse 25.

63. *Ibid.*, verses 21-22. There was some confusion over the precise location of the "Miḥrāb of David" for which see G. Le Strange, *Palestine under the Moslems, op. cit.*, 167-169; 171, 212.

64. Concerning the significance of this account see J. W. Hirschberg, *op. cit.*, 319-320. The influence of Rajā' on the selection of 'Umar II as Caliph can be seen in the account of Bal'amī, *Chronique*, IV, 236-238.

65. Ṭabarī, *Ta'rīkh*, I/6, 2408, line 11.

66. *Ibid.*, lines 11-15.

67. *Ibid.*, 2408, line 15; 2409, line 1.

68. *Ibid.*, 2409, lines 2-11.

69. *Ibid.*, lines 12-16.

70. M. Canard, "Les expéditions des Arabes contre Constantinople dans l'histoire et dans la légende," *Journal Asiatique* 208-209 (1926), 67-70.

71. *Ibid.*, 80-94, and 99-102.

72. Concerning legends created to connect Sulaymān the 'Umayyad with Solomon, see *ibid.*, 107.

73. al-Bīrūnī, *Āthār*, 212, *Chronology*, 196.

74. For the date of the Dome of the Rock see Creswell, E.M.A.[2], I/1, 69, 72-73. The suggestion that the Dome of the Rock was intended to commemorate the "Ascension" of the Prophet and thereby to replace the Kaaba has been discarded by most scholars. Goitein, "Sanctity of Jerusalem," *op. cit.*, 135-140,

and Grabar, "The 'Umayyad Dome of the Rock," *op. cit.*, 34-38.

75. For documentary evidence see Creswell, E.M.A.², I/2, 373-374; for archaeological evidence see *ibid.*, 378-380.

76. Grabar, "The 'Umayyad Dome of the Rock," *op. cit.*, 56-58.

77. *Ibid.*, 52-55.

78. *Ibid.*, 61-62.

79. The evidence collected by Kister suggests that by the late seventh century Jerusalem was regarded as one of the holiest shrines in the world. The excessive veneration of Jerusalem stimulated the circulation of traditions which attempted to stem popular enthusiasm for the site. The anti-Jerusalem traditions appear to have been created in the early eighth century. (Kister, "You shall set out only for Three Mosques," *op. cit.*, 173-196). Characteristically, the texts collected by Ibn al-Faqīh in the Kitāb al-Buldān not only include references to the miracles associated with Jerusalem in Jewish traditions, but also traditions attributed to the Prophet Muhammad, and references to the Prophet's Night Journey. Although a complete study of the contents of this passage has not been made, some of the authorities cited appear to be of the 'Umayyad period. *(Kitāb al-Buldān,* 95:1-6 for the Three Mosques tradition; 101:8-14 for places connected with the Prophet's Night Journey).

80. There is a possible implicit comparison in the poetry of Jalāl al-Dīn Rūmī which will be discussed below. See *The Mathnawi of Jalalu'ddin Rumi*, ed. R. A. Nicholson (London, 1930), text, book 4, lines 467-475.

81. Creswell, E.M.A.², I/1, plate 5a shows the inner face of the octagonal zone and the outer face of the circular one.

82. *Ibid.*, plates 6-9 and 35a, also R. Ettinghausen, *Arab Painting* (Geneva, 1962), 18.

83. Creswell, E.M.A.², I/1, plates 11, 12, 14, 15, 17, 18, 20, 21.

84. *Ibid.*, naturalistic trees and plants: 11a, 15b, 17c; trees with jeweled trunks: 14a, b; 15c, 12b, c.

85. *Ibid.*, plates 11c, 17b, 18b, c, 20b, c, 21b, c.

86. See above note 54.

87. *Yoma* 21b, 39b. See Ginzberg, *op. cit.*, VI, 294, n. 58.

88. Some of them are grape vines: *Ibid.*, plates 11, 14, 15; others are acanthus scrolls, plates 18, 20, 21; while two (plates 14, 15) resemble the foliage of pomegranate bushes.

89. For jeweled stems see *ibid.*, plates 14, 15; jeweled fruits are seen on plates 17, 18; crowns on plates 18, 20, 21.

90. *Ibid.*, plates 13, 16, 19, 22.

91. For a color plate, see *ibid.*, 35b; and Ettinghausen, *Arab Painting, op. cit.*, 23.

92. See above notes 49 and 50.

93. Creswell, E.M.A.², I/1, plates 23-26.

94. *Ibid.*, plates 24b, f; 25b, c.

95. *Ibid.*, for garlands: plates 23a, c, d, 25b, f, 26d, e; for cornucopias: plates 25a, d, e, 26b; and figs. 237-247, 271.

96. von Berchem, *ibid.*, 269.

97. Muḥammad b. Aḥmad al-Muqaddasī, *Aḥsan al-Taqāsīm fī Ma'rifat al-Aqālīm*, ed. M. J. de Goeje (Leiden, 1906), 173, lines 10-12; and al-Muqaddasī, *Aḥsan al-Taqāsīm*, trans. A. Miquel (Damascus, 1963), 202.

98. Al-Muqaddasī, 166:15-17; al-Muqaddasī, 187.

99. For a general discussion and basic bibliography see B. Schrieke "Isrā'" and J. Horovitz, "Mi'rādj" in E. I.¹.

100. A. Guillaume, "Where was al-Masyid al-Aqsa?", *Al-Andalus* 18 (1953), 327-333.

101. Horovitz, "Mi'rādj", E. I.¹

102. Although the date and authenticity of the early references to Masjid al-Aqṣā as Jerusalem have not yet been established, sources cited include: the poets 'Umar ibn Abī Rabī'a, and Abū Sakhr (in Horovitz, "Mi'rādj" E. I.¹); Hudayfa ibn al-Yaman, d. 656, and Zirr ibn al-Hubaysh, d. 702 (in Hirschberg, *op. cit.*, 337-338); Raja' ibn Haywah (in Ṭabarī, *Ta'rīkh*, I/6, 2408) and Ḥasan al-Baṣrī, d. 768 and Qatāda ibn Di'āma, d. 735, cited by Ibn Isḥāq (d. 768) in his book on the life of the Prophet Muhammad which is preserved in the edition of Ibn Hishām, d. 828 or 833 [*Kitāb Sīrat Rasūl Allāh*, ed. F. Wüstenfeld I (Göttingen, 1858), 268-271].

103. Goitein, "Sanctity of Jerusalem," *op. cit.*, 143-144.

104. *Ibid.*, 140-141.

105. In his Quranic commentary Ṭabarī explains "Masjid al-Aqṣā" as "Masjid Bayt al-Muqaddas" remarking that it was called the "furthermost" because it was the most distant of the mosques which are visited (*Jāmi' al-Bayān*, XV, 5). This is an apparent reference to the tradition "You shall only set out for Three Mosques" studied by Kister. (see above notes 22, 79).

106. Hirschberg, *op. cit.*, 322.

107. Ibn Isḥaq/Ibn Hishām, *Kitāb Sīrat Rasūl Allāh*, I, 264; a

translation of the passage is in A. Guillaume, *The Life of Muhammad, op. cit.*, 182.

108. Ibn Isḥāq/Ibn Hishām, I, 264-265; Guillaume, *Life of Muhammad, op. cit.*, 182-183.

109. Bibliothèque Nationale, Paris, Ms. suppl. turc. 190, fol. 7, 840/1436; for a general discussion of this manuscript see I. Stchoukine, *Les peintures des manuscrits tîmurîdes* (Paris, 1954), 54-55.

110. See above notes 13, 18.

111. Al-Muqaddasī, 168, lines 5-8; also al-Muqaddasī, trans. Miquel, 190-191.

112. For example, in the text of 'Alī al-Harawī (d. 1215) it is called "Masjid al-Aqṣā" and he notes an inscription in the dome of the structure quoting the verse describing the "Isrā'" (i.e. Sura 17:1), which bears the date of 426/1035. (*Kitāb al-Ishārāt*, 25-26).

113. Istanbul, Topkapï Sarayï Müzesi Kütüphanesi, Hazine 2154, fol. 62. Although originally the painting probably illustrated a text dealing with the Prophet's ascension, it is preserved in an album of calligraphy and paintings; see R. Ettinghausen, "Persian Ascension Miniatures of the Fourteenth Century" *Accademia Nazionale dei Lincei*, Atti XII (Rome, 1957), 364-366, fig. 2.

114. Jerusalem was frequently visited by Iranian ascetics and mystics, although the texts describing their visits have not yet been analyzed to extract their descriptions of the Dome of the Rock. For references see Goitein, "The Sanctity of Jerusalem" *op. cit.*, 142-143. The description of the Dome of the Rock given by Ibn al-Faqīh refers to the use of marble

and gold in the structure. He also states that "the Rock" is in the center of the building. (*Kitāb al-Buldān*, 100:14-101:5).

115. Ḥamd Allāh Mustawfī, *The Geographical Part of Nuzhat al-Qulūb*, 16, lines 19-20.

116. Jalāl al-Dīn Rūmī, *Mathnawī-i Ma'nawī*, Bk. 4, lines 467-474.

117. Dīnawarī, *Akhbār al-Ṭiwāl*, 19, lines 5-6; also Ibn Isḥāq/Ibn Hishām, I, 266, Guillaume, *Life of Muhammad, op. cit.*, 183 and Ṭabarī, *Jāmi' al-Bayān*, XV, 6.

118. Istanbul, Topkapî Sarayî Müzesi Kütüphanesi, Hazine 2154, fol. 107; Ettinghausen, "Persian Ascension Miniatures," *op. cit.*, figs. 8-9, where it is identified as "The Vision of the Conquest of Constantinople" (*ibid.*, 373, 376).

119. Ṭabarī, *Jāmi' al-Bayān*, XV, 110.

120. *Ibid.*, 112.

121. Ibn Isḥāq/Ibn Hishām, I, 264-65, Guillaume, *Life of Muhammad, op. cit.*, 183.

122. Ṭabarī, *Jāmi' al-Bayān*, XV, 6. The remark is placed in the discussion of Sura 17, verse 1.

123. Istanbul, Millet Kütüphanesi, F. 44, fols. 60v-96.

124. *Ibid.*, fols. 93v-94.

125. *Ibid.*, fols. 95-95v.

126. B. Schrieke, "Die Himmelsreise Muhammeds," *Der Islam* 6 (1916), 15-16.

127. Zakariyā' b. Muḥammad al-Qazwīnī, *Āthār al-Bilād* (Beirut, 1960), 160-161. Also al-Muqaddasī, 167-168; and al-Muqaddasī, 189-190.

128. See above note 25.

129. Ibn al-Faqīh, *Kitāb al-Buldān*, 95, lines 15-18. For the wider significance of these traditions see Hirschberg, *op. cit.*, 326, 329.

THE MESSIANIC TEMPLE IN SPANISH MEDIEVAL HEBREW MANUSCRIPTS

Joseph Gutmann

Despite the fact that the Temple of Solomon is frequently mentioned in rabbinic literature, it first makes its symbolic appearance in Jewish pictorial art in thirteenth-century Spanish Hebrew manuscripts.[1] The only earlier depiction that may possibly represent the Temple of Solomon is a late Roman temple structure on a mural panel of the third-century Dura synagogue.[2]

Attempts of scholars to identify schematic renderings of cult utensils in tenth-eleventh-century Muslim Hebrew manuscripts as those belonging to the Temple of Solomon have not been convincing. These illustrations in Muslim Hebrew manuscripts clearly show not the Temple of Solomon, but the wilderness Tabernacle.[3] The many synagogue mosaics that have been found, dating from the fourth to the sixth century, reveal the Torah ark with the symbols of the Jewish holidays.[4] These depictions do not form a continuous tradition of Temple representations leading directly to the Spanish manuscript images, as has been maintained.[5]

It became customary in Spain from the late thirteenth century on to adorn Hebrew Bible manuscripts with depictions of the cult objects that, according to rabbinic tradition, once graced the ancient Solomonic Temple. Some twenty Spanish Hebrew Bible manuscripts containing this unique iconography have survived from the thirteenth to the fifteenth centuries.[6] Frequently illuminated in gold and silver and carefully arranged in compartments, these cult appurtenances are usually spread over two folios, although there are some exceptions.[7] These illustrations most often appear on the preliminary folios preceding the Hebrew Bibles rather than accompanying the descriptive passages of these cult objects in the books of Exodus, Leviticus and Numbers, as is the usual procedure in both Christian and Hebrew manuscripts. It is not clear when the practice of placing these images on the preliminary folios first arose. The earliest manuscript that has come down to us picturing the Sanctuary vessels is from Perpignan of the kingdom of Aragon (fig. 34), and is dated 1299 (Bibliothèque Nationale, MS hebr. 7, fols. 12v-13).[8] It depicts the golden lampstand (*menorah*, Ex. 25.31ff., Ex. 37.17ff., and Num. 8.4), its tongs (*malkahayim*) and snuffers (*mahtot*, Ex. 25.38 and Ex. 37.23), the jar of manna (*tzintzenet ha-man*, Ex. 16.33) flanked by the barren rod (*mateh*) and the budding rod of Aaron (Num. 17.18, 23), the cherubim (*keruvim*)[9] seated on the ark cover (*kapporet*, Ex. 25.18, 20; Ex. 37.9), the table of showbread (*shulhan ha-tahor*, Ex. 25.23-30 and Lev. 24.6) and the tablets of the Ten Commandments. It should be noted that the opening Hebrew words of each Commandment are given (Ex. 20 and Deut. 5). As the opening word of the Fourth Commandment varies in the two versions, *zakhor* (remember, Ex. 20.8) and *shamor* (observe, Deut. 5.12) the Sabbath, both are inserted.[10] On folio 13 (fig. 35) we see the golden incense altar (*mizbah haketoret*, Ex. 30.1; Ex. 30.27; Ex. 39.38; Ex. 40.26),[11] with the two silver trumpets (*hatzotzrot*, Num. 10.2) and the horn (*shofar*, Lev. 25.9) underneath it. In the left compartment is the altar of burnt offering (*mizbah ha-olah*, Ex. 27.1ff.; Ex. 30.28; Ex. 38.1ff., Ex. 39.39), its copper grating of meshwork (*ma'aseh reshet*, Ex. 27.4; Ex. 38.4) and the laver (*kiyyor*) and its stand (*kan*, Ex. 30.18; Ex. 39.39). At the bottom are the pots (*sirot*) for the ashes, the basins (*mizrakot*) for the blood of the sacrifices, the triangular shovels or scrapers (*ya'im*) for the removal of ashes, the flesh-hooks (*mizlagot*) for turning the broiling meat, and the firepans (*mahtot*) to carry the hot coals (Ex. 27.3; Ex. 38.3).

Although these cult utensils are mentioned in the Bible, others illustrated here are not—for example, the two pans of frankincense (*bazikhei levonah*),[12] the stone (*even*) with three steps standing next to the lampstand[13] and the ramp (*kevesh*) leading up to the altar.[14] However, these additional objects, as well as the arrangement of the loaves of showbread in compartments on the table[15] and the decorative elements of the lampstand[16] with its six flames turning to the central flame[17] closely follow the description found in the eighth book (*Avodah*, the Book of Temple Service) of the *Mishneh Torah*, the legal code of the twelfth-century philosopher Maimonides. What is the explanation for the insertion of these images on the opening pages of Spanish Hebrew Bibles?

One clue lies in the inscription to folio 13 of our miniature, which reads:

> All [implements existed] while the Temple was upon its site and the holy Sanctuary was upon its foundation.
> Blessed is he who beheld the splendor of the beauty of its greatness and all the acts of its power and its might.
> And happy is he who hopes and lives to see it.
> May it be Your will that it [the Temple] be speedily rebuilt in our days so that our eyes may behold it and our heart rejoice.

In another manuscript (Modena, Biblioteca Estense, Cod. M. 8.4, fol. 10) the border inscription around the Temple utensils uses the words "before the inner sanctuary (*devir*)." *Devir* is not encountered in the Pentateuch and is found only in Kings and in Chronicles, where it always refers to the Holy of Holies in Solomon's Temple.[18]

Don Samuel ha-Levi Abulafia, chief treasurer of King Pedro I of Castile, who around 1357 built the magnificent synagogue in Toledo, known today as El Tránsito, also expressed in the inscriptions of his synagogue's eastern wall the ardent hope that he might "see the rebuilding of the Temple" so that he and his sons might forever minister in it.[19]

Furthermore, Maimonides, the most influential and widely read Spanish Jewish philosopher, emphasizes the Temple in his legal code in the same way that the Spanish

Bible manuscripts and Samuel he-Levi do. Maimonides' rational mind rejected and scorned such naive notions, held by his contemporary German brethren, as feasting in the Garden of Eden in the messianic age. The Temple, he argued, would be rebuilt in the messianic period when a Jewish kingdom, ruled by Jewish law, would be established in the land of Israel under a King-Messiah.[20]

The Spanish Jew of the Middle Ages adhered to the Maimonidian belief, which he also uttered daily in his prayers:

> May it be Your will that the Temple be speedily rebuilt in our days.

To strengthen and insure this fervent desire to behold the Temple in the messianic future, he placed in his Bibles a visual image of the Sanctuary vessels which, according to tradition, were hidden by king Josiah, the prophet Jeremiah or God himself, but would be restored in messianic times.[21]

Where do the models for such depictions of the Temple implements lie? As we indicated there is little connection between these cultic utensils in Spanish Hebrew manuscripts and earlier Jewish art. Similarly, few iconographic or stylistic parallels can be deduced from Christian art. The seventh-century Codex Amiatinus, the eleventh to thirteenth century Byzantine Octateuchs and twelfth-century Western manuscripts do feature the cult appurtenances of the wilderness Tabernacle, but they offer hardly any convincing similarities. It would appear then that these representations are unique expressions of the theology and philosophy of Spanish Judaism. Early Christianity had no interest in the Jewish Messianic Temple, as the Temple of Jerusalem was destroyed according to the prophesies of Jesus (Matthew 24.1-2; Mark 13.1-2; Luke 21.5-6) and would not be rebuilt. The later medieval church, for its part, was sometimes called the "New Solomonic Temple" in fulfillment of Jesus' prophesies and hence precluded the necessity of a messianic temple.[22] The artistic models, however, are not unique, for some of the vessels in our Spanish miniatures can be found in Muslim art, as can be seen from a page of al-Jazarī's thirteenth-century *Book of Knowledge of Mechanical Contrivances*, known as the *Treatise on Automata*. A miniature from this manuscript made for the king of Amida, Northern Mesopotamia, around 1315, shows an automaton with a female figure holding an ewer with dragon spout (fig. 36), that resembles the laver with dragon spouts on folio 13.[23]

The Perpignan Bible illuminations or their immediate models established an iconographic tradition which we can pursue in several early fourteenth-century Spanish Hebrew Bible manuscripts.[24] Distinct iconographic variations on this tradition begin to appear in Spanish Hebrew Bible manuscripts from the second quarter of the fourteenth century on. Several of these manuscripts are closely related, and fortunately one of them is dated 1336 [figs. 37-38] (Istanbul, Karaite synagogue, Pentateuch, pages 18-19). In these manuscripts, we usually find that the lampstand is placed on a separate folio and that the tablets of the Ten

Commandments are often divided horizontally and outfitted with the prescribed four rings and two poles (*taba'ot* and *badim*, Ex. 25.12,15). The barren rod, the incense pans and the cherubim are frequently eliminated, while the laver usually looks like a large chalice rather than a dragon-spouted ewer.[25]

To further underscore the association of the cultic implements with the Temple, we find that some manuscripts introduce musical instruments such as the lyre, harp and cymbal, since the Levis used them to perform in the Temple service.[26] Two manuscripts place next to the appurtenances a building, no doubt meant to represent the Temple.[27] In another manuscript, the pillars *Jakhin* and *Bo'az* (I Kings 7.15-22), are found amidst the Sanctuary utensils, so that no mistake can be made that we are dealing with the Temple of Solomon.[28]

Perhaps the most important innovation in these manuscripts is the depiction of a mound which frequently has one stylized tree atop it. In two manuscripts, this mound is even identified as the Mount of Olives (*har ha-zeitim*).[29] What is the meaning of the Mount of Olives amidst the Sanctuary vessels? One manuscript, dated 1404 from Saragossa, Spain (Bibliothèque Nationale, MS hebr. 31, fol. 4) has a whole page devoted to the Mount of Olives (fig. 39). Around the illustration of the mount runs an inscription from Zechariah 14.4:

> And His feet shall stand on that day on the Mount of Olives which lies before Jerusalem on the east; and the

Mount of Olives shall be split in two from east to west by a very wide valley . . .

Rabbinic literature clarifies the enigmatic association of the Mount of Olives with the Temple. According to these sources, the Almighty will make caverns in the earth and will cause the righteous dead who die during the dispersion to roll underground until they emerge at the Mount of Olives on the day of resurrection.[30] Moreover, the high priest, who used to stand on the Mount of Olives while performing the red heifer ceremony, was able to look from there directly into the entrance of the Temple sanctuary (*Mishnah, Middot* 2.4).[31] Hence it becomes clear why the Mount of Olives is depicted amidst the Temple utensils in Spanish Hebrew manuscripts. It was to underscore the belief that, upon resurrection at the Mount of Olives in Jerusalem in messianic times, the righteous dead, like the high priest of old, would be able to view from that vantage point the beautiful objects in the rebuilt Messianic Temple.[32]

Furthermore, Holy Scripture—the Hebrew Bible—itself came to be called in fourteenth-century Spain "Sanctuary of God" (*mikdashiyah*). Its threefold division [Torah (Pentateuch)-Prophets-Writings (Hagiography)] was likened to the three divisions of the ancient Temple.[33]

When the Spanish Jew included representations of the Sanctuary utensils on the opening folios of his Bible, he was giving visual expression to his ardent hope and belief that he would view the restored Temple—with all its splendid appurtenances—in the messianic future.

1. Cf. "Temple in Rabbinical Literature," *The Jewish Encyclopedia* XII (New York, 1906), 92-97.
2. Cf. J. Gutmann, ed., *The Dura-Europos Synagogue, A Reevaluation* (Missoula, Montana, 1973), 142.
   A temple-like structure found on the Torah shrine in the Dura synagogue and a similar design found on Jewish coins of the Second Revolt under Hadrian has been interpreted as representing the Temple of Solomon or the Temple of Herod with the Ark of the Covenant. Other scholars feel that the building is a synagogue with its Torah shrine. Neither interpretation is convincing, as historic and archaeological evidence is insufficient for this period to warrant any far reaching conclusions. Cf. C. H. Kraeling, *The Synagogue* (New Haven, 1956), 60-61; B. Kanael, "Altjüdische Münzen," *Jahrbuch für Numismatik und Geldgeschichte* 17 (1967), 184ff. Cf. also S. Ferber, "The Pre-Constantinian Shrine of St. Peter: Jewish Sources and Christian Aftermath," *Gesta* 10 (1971), 8-9.
3. Cf. J. Gutmann, "The Illustrated Jewish Manuscript in Antiquity: The Present State of the Question," *Gesta* 5 (1966), 40-41 and J. Gutmann, ed., *No Graven Images: Studies in Art and the Hebrew Bible* (New York, 1971), 234-35.
   It is probable that the three arched gates and the two ornamented sections with triangular tops in between the gates may represent the 5 columns or posts for the curtain or screen which stood at the entrance to the Tabernacle (Ex. 26.37 and 36.38). This interpretation is strengthened by the five column bases which are clearly depicted in a related page of the same manuscript. Cf. M. Metzger, "Quelques caractères iconographiques et ornementaux de deux manuscrits hébraiques du Xe siècle," *Cahiers de civilisation médiévale* 1 (1958), 205ff., and B. Narkiss, *Hebrew Illuminated Manuscripts* (Jerusalem, 1969), 42.

4. Cf. B. Kanael, *Die Kunst der antiken Synagoge* (Munich, 1961).

5. The arguments proposed by Roth and Nordström are refuted in T. Metzger, "Les objets du culte, le sanctuaire du désert et le Temple de Jérusalem, dans les bibles hebraïques médiévales enluminées, en Orient et en Espagne," *Bulletin of the John Rylands Library* 52 (1970), 399ff.

6. The following is a list of known Spanish Hebrew manuscripts with depictions of the cult objects of the Messianic Temple. All references in this paper will refer to the particular manuscript according to the number assigned to it here.

(1). Paris, Bibliothèque Nationale, Ms. hebr. 7, folios 12v-13. Written by Solomon ben Raphael for himself in Perpignan, Aragon, 1299. Verses from Num. 8.4 and Ex. 25.34 around 12v, *Avodah*, Yom Kippur, Esther 1.4, 10.2, Daniel 12.12 and daily *Amidah* around folio 13. *Synagoga*, Catalog of exhibition held at Historisches Museum, Frankfurt am/Main (Frankfurt am/Main, 1961), "Handschriften," No. 75; C. O. Nordström, "Some Miniatures in Hebrew Bibles," *Synthronon* (Paris, 1968), 90-93; T. Metzger, "Les objets du culte, le sanctuaire du désert et le Temple de Jérusalem, dans les bibles hebraïques médiévales enluminées, en Orient et en Espagne," *Bulletin of the John Rylands Library* 52 (1970), 419-20.

(2). Parma, Biblioteca Palatina, Ms. Parm. 2668 (de Rossi 782), fols. 7v-8, Spain, early 14th century (The ms. itself was written in Toledo in 1277). Verses from Prov. 2.3-11; 3.1-3.
Manoscritti biblici ebraici decorati, Catalog of exhibition held at Biblioteca Trivulziana, Milan (Milan, 1966), No. 32, 77-78, plates 24-25; Nordström, *op. cit.*, 89, 95; Metzger, *op. cit.*, 416-19.

(3). Copenhagen, Det Kongelige Bibliotek, Cod. Hebr. II, fols. 11v-12, Catalonia, 1301. Verses from Num. 8.4 and Ex. 25.34 and Lev. 24.6 around 11v. *Avodah*, Yom Kippur, Esther 1.4, 10.2, Daniel 12.12 and daily *Amidah* around folio 12.

C. Roth, "Jewish Antecedents of Christian Art," *Journal of the Warburg and Courtauld Institutes* 16 (1953), plate 6; *Synagoga, op. cit.*, No. 78 (Color plate of fol. 12, fig. 43); Metzger, *op. cit.*, 420-22.

(4). Modena, Biblioteca Estense, Cod. M. 8.4, fols. 9v, 10, 11, Catalonia (?), early 14th century. Verses are not taken literally but adapted primarily from Ex. 25.31, 38, Ex. 27.3, Num. 17.23, II Chron. 4.20, Ex. 40.26, 29, Num. 10.2, Ex. 30.18, Ex. 27.3, Ex. 37.9, Ex. 31.18. *Manoscritti, op. cit.* No. 33, 78-80, plate 26 (11v); C. Bernheimer, *Catalogo dei manoscritti orientali della Biblioteca Estense* (Rome, 1960), No. 2, 4-6; Metzger, *op. cit.*, 422-26, plate II.

(5). New York, private collection (formerly Frankfurt, Stadtbibliothek, Ausst. 4), fols. 25v-26, Spain, first quarter, 14th century. Verses from Ex. 25.31-34, 39.

G. Swarzenski and R. Schilling, *Die illuminierten Handschriften und Einzelminiaturen des Mittelalters in Frankfurter Besitz* I (Frankfurt am/Main, 1929), No. 48, 50-51; II, plate XXIX; Nordström, *op. cit.* 96, figs. 13-14; Metzger, *op. cit.*, 426ff.

(6). Modena, Biblioteca Estense, Cod. T.3.8, fols. 25v-26, Catalonia (?), first quarter of 14th century. Verses from Ex. 25.31-34, 39.

Bernheimer, *op. cit.*, No. 3, 6-9; L. Mortara Ottolenghi, "Il manoscritto T.3.8 della Biblioteca Estense di Modena e la sua decorazione," *Rassegna Mensile di Israel* 36 (1970), 260ff.; Metzger, *op. cit.*, 426ff., plate II.

(7). Istanbul, Karaite synagogue in Hasköy, pages 18-19, Spain, 1336 (Pentateuch only). Verses from Ex. 37.17-18, Ex. 38.3-4. Written by Samuel ben ?.
I. Ben-Zvi, "'Mikdashiyah' of Jerusalem and Bible Manuscripts in Karaite Synagogues of Istanbul and Egypt," *Kiryath Sepher* 32 (1957), 368-69, plate 3 (Hebrew). I am greatly indebted to Mr. Albert Sonsino for examining this manuscript and informing me that Ben-Zvi confused the two manuscripts. Cf. also L. A. Mayer, *L'art juif en terre de l'Islam* (Geneva, 1959), plate 18 (wrongly identified as a Karaite ms. on p. 27).

(8). London, British Museum, Harl. 1528, fols. 7-7v, Spain, second quarter of 14th century.
Nordström, *op. cit.*, 93f., figs. 7-8; Metzger, *op. cit.* 53 (1970), 175ff.

(9). London, British Museum, Add. 15250, fols. 3v-4, Spain, second quarter of 14th century.
Nordström, *op. cit.*, 95, figs. 9-10; Metzger, *op. cit.*, 178ff.

(10). Parma, Biblioteca Palatina, Ms. Parm. 2810 (de Rossi 518), fols. 7v-8, Spain, second quarter of 14th century.
Metzger, *op. cit.*, 170ff., plate III.

(11). Istanbul, Karaite synagogue in Hasköy, fols. 3v-4, Spain, second quarter of 14th century (Pentateuch only). Verses from Num. 8.4, Ex. 39.36, Ex. 31.8, 25.38, 37.24.
Ben-Zvi, *op. cit.*, 369; Cf. A. Danon, "Documents relating to the History of the Karaites in European Turkey," *Jewish Quarterly Review*, N.S. 17 (1926-1927), 190-92. I am indebted to Mr. Albert Sonsino for kindly obtaining a photo of these folios for me.

(11[a]). Cairo, Karaite synagogue, Spain, 14th century (?).
R. Gottheil, "Some Hebrew Manuscripts in Cairo,"

Jewish Quarterly Review, O.S. 17 (1905), 630-31. Ms. Leila Avrin kindly informed that the ms. is probably from the 14th century, but I have been unable to obtain a photo of the folios.

(12). Milan, Biblioteca Ambrosiana, Cod. 105 Sup., fols. Iv-II, Spain, second half of 14th century (Pentateuch and Joshua). Verses from Psalms 19.8-9, 119.97; Prov. 8.22, 8.11; Deut. 33.4.
Metzger, *op. cit.*, 196ff.; A. Luzzatto and L. Mortara Ottolenghi, *Hebraica Ambrosiana* (Milan, 1972), 129-32.

(13). Paris, Bibliothèque Nationale, Ms. hebr. 31, fols. lv, 2v, 3, 4, Saragossa, Spain, 1404. Written by Hayyim ben Saul, called Vital Satori. The same scribe wrote No. 16 (Sassoon Ms. 16). Verses from Num. 8.4; Ex. 25.32, 35; Lev. 24.5-6; Prov. 8.22-24, 26-29; Zechariah 14.4-5. Metzger, *op. cit.*, 199ff., plate IV.

(14). Rome, Comunità Israelitica, No. 19, fols. 214v and 216, Spain, 14th century, Pentateuch (The ms. itself was written in Barcelona, 1325). Verses from Job 28.16, 19, 23; Prov. 3.13, 6.23, 3.2, 7.2.
Manoscritti biblici, op. cit., No. 50, 98-99; Metzger, *op. cit.*, 182ff.

(15). Letchworth, Herts., Private collection of Rabbi S. D. Sassoon, Ms. 368 (Farhi Bible), pp. 182-183, 186-187, Catalonia (?), 1366-1382. Scribe and artist (?): Elisha ben Abraham ben Beveniste ben Elisha Crescas.
D. S. Sassoon, Ohel Dawid, *Descriptive Catalogue of the Hebrew and Samaritan Manuscripts in the Sassoon Library* (London, 1932), I, 6-14; J. Leveen, *The Hebrew Bible in Art* (London, 1944), 109-12, plates XXXV-XXXVI; B. Narkiss, *Hebrew Illuminated Manuscripts* (Jerusalem, 1969), 72; Metzger, *op. cit.*, 188ff., plate III.

(16). Letchworth, Herts., Private collection of Rabbi S. D. Sassoon, Ms. 16 (RSBA Bible), pp. 6-7, Cervera, 1383. Same scribe as No. 13 (Paris, B.N., Ms. hebr. 31). Sassoon, *op. cit.*, I, 14-15, Metzger, *op. cit.*, 192ff., plate III.

(17). Jerusalem, Jewish National and University Library, Ms. 8º5147, fol. 6v, Spain, second half of 14th century (?). Verses from Deut. 4.44, Malachi 3.22.
Manuscripts and Rare Books. Catalog of exhibition from the Collections of the Jewish National and University Library (Jerusalem, 1970), XVI, No. 6.

(18). London, British Museum, Kings I, fols. 3, 3v, 4, Salsona, Spain, 1385. Verses from Num. 8.4, Prov. 6.23, Psalms 19.8-11, Prov. 16.24, 3.8 and Psalms 119.103. Nordström, *op. cit.*, 92, figs. 5-6; Metzger, *op. cit.*, 194ff.

(19). Paris, Bibliothèque Nationale, Ms. hebr. 1314, fols. 1v-2, Spain, late 14th or 15th century (?). Verses from Num. 8.4; Ex. 25.39; Ex. 30.27; Ex. 25.38-40.
Synagoga, op. cit., No. 88, fig. 47 (1v); Metzger, *op. cit.*, 203ff.

(20). Oxford, Bodleian Library, Ms. Kennicott I, fols. 120v-121, La Coruña, Spain, 1476.
C. Roth, *The Kennicott Bible* (Oxford, 1957), 8 and plate 8; Nordström, *op. cit.*, 98, figs. 17, 19; Metzger, *op. cit.*, 207ff.; Narkiss, *op. cit.*, 74.

7. Some of the cult objects are spread over three folios (Modena, Biblioteca Estense, Cod. M. 8.4 and British Museum, Kings I), while in other manuscripts they are spread over 4 folios (Letchworth, Private collection of Rabbi Sassoon, Ms. 368 and Paris, Bibliothèque Nationale, Ms. Hebr. 31). See Nos. 4, 18, 15, 13 in note 6.

8. It is highly doubtful that No. 2 (footnote 6) was illuminated in

JOSEPH GUTMANN

1277. Cf. Metzger, *op. cit.*, 418 and Nordström, *op. cit.*, 95. The cult objects are crudely executed and seem to copy those of No. 1 or its model. Unlike other miniatures of this iconographic type, the inscriptions around the border bear no relation to the cult objects shown—an indication that it was probably not originally intended for these pages. Furthermore, the established iconography of the Temple vessels, as can be seen in Nos. 1, 3, 4, is not followed and the objects are arbitrarily dispersed within the frame.

9. The winged cherubim are shown as bearded youths, since Ibn Ezra in his Commentary to Ex. 25.18 mentions that they have the face of a youth. Cf. also Maimonides, *Guide for the Perplexed,* Part III, Chap. 1 for a similar explanation. Cf. Babylonian Talmud, *Sukkah* 5b.

10. *Zakhor-shamor* is also found in Nos. 3 and 4, note 6. It appears in the 14th-century Peter Comestor manuscript (Madrid, Bibl. Nac., Cod. Res. 199), which provides an interesting example of a Jewish iconographic tradition copied in a Christian Spanish manuscript. Cf. C. O. Nordström, "The Temple Miniatures in the Peter Comestor Manuscript at Madrid," *Horae Soederblomianae* 6 (1964), 54ff. Cf. Babylonian Talmud, *Shevuot* 20b.
To the many iconographic parallels cited by Nordström, the following can be added:
The winged cherubim are found in Nos. 3, 4 (note 6). The budding rod of Aaron is similar to that in Nos. 15, 18. The shovels as brooms are also found in Nos. 11, 14, 15, 18, 19. The fleshhooks are similar to those depicted in Nos. 8, 11, 15 and the enclosed shelves on the table of showbread are similar to those in Nos. 9, 10, 11. In most manuscripts from the second quarter of the fourteenth century, the grating of meshwork has been eliminated, as in this manuscript.

11. The golden altar (*mizbah ha-zahav*) mentioned in the Bible is identical to the altar of incense (*mizbah ha-ketoret*).

12. Maimonides, *Mishneh Torah*, Book VIII (*Avodah*, "The Book of Temple Service"), Treatise I, Chapter 3.15 and Treatise VI, Chapter 5.4. This interpretation is based on Lev. 24.7 which mentions that "pure frankincense" is to be placed with the loaves of showbread. Cf. also *Mishnah, Yoma* 2.5 and *Tamid* 2.5. Metzger, *op. cit.*, 417, n. 1 claims that the word *khappotav* (Ex. 25.29) means incense pans. This cannot be substantiated, as the meaning of the biblical word is uncertain. Cf. H. M. Orlinsky, *Notes on the New Translation of The Torah* (Philadelphia, 1969), 187.

13. Only one stone with three steps is cited in the sources. The two stones appear in our miniatures, no doubt, for the sake of symmetry. The priest would trim the lamps of the menorah while standing on the steps of this stone. Cf. Maimonides, *op. cit.*, I, 3.11 and *Mishnah, Tamid* 3.9.

14. Maimonides, *op. cit.*, I, 1.17. Cf. *Mishnah, Yoma* 2.1 and *Zebahim* 9.7.

15. Maimonides, *op. cit.*, 3.13-15; VI, 5.2. Cf. *Mishnah, Menahot* 11.5-6.

16. Maimonides, *op. cit.*, I, 3.

17. *Ibid.*, I, 8.3. Cf. also *Sifre* to Numbers 8.2, par. 59.

18. Metzger, *op. cit.*, 432, plate II, fig. 3. Cf. J. Ouellette, "The Solomonic debîr according to the Hebrew Text of I Kings 6," *Journal of Biblical Literature* 89 (1970), 338ff.

19. F. Cantera Burgos, *Sinagogas españolas* (Madrid, 1955), 123 and fig. 25a.

20. *Mishneh Torah*, Book XIV, Chapters 11-12. Cf. S. Zeitlin, *Maimonides, A Biography* (New York, 1958), 24ff. and 151ff. Cf. also *Targum*, Song of Songs 1.17.

21. Isaac ben Judah Abravanel, Commentary to II Kings 23, par. 670. Cf. *Midrash Tanhuma*, Numbers, 50; Babylonian Talmud, *Yoma* 52b, 54a; *Horayot* 12a. Cf. J. Sarachek, *The Doctrine of the Messiah in Medieval Jewish Literature* (New York, 1932), 294 and L. Ginzberg, *The Legends of the Jews* (Philadelphia, 1947), III, 48, 158, 161; IV, 234, 282, 320; VI, 19, n. 112; 65, n. 332; 66, n. 341; 377, n. 118; 410, n. 61, VI, 442, n. 36. Cf. also the interesting inscription on a tombstone from Toledo, Spain, 1315:
"How awesome is this place; here a vision of God can be contemplated by every man who inclines his heart to see it. For in it are hidden the vessels of the Sanctuary, the sacrificial altar and the ark of Israel. F. Cantera Burgos and J. Millás Vallicrosa, *Las inscripciones hebraicas de España* (Madrid, 1956), 85ff. Cf. also 20, 63, 125, 144, 157, and M. F. Collins, "The Hidden Vessels in Samaritan Traditions," *Journal for the Study of Judaism* 3 (1972), 97-116.

22. Typologically, such Temple/Tabernacle vessels as the menorah, rod of Aaron, jar of manna were seen as types or prefigurations of Christ or the Virgin. Cf. P. Bloch, "Siebenarmige Leuchter in christlichen Kirchen," *Wallraf-Richartz Jahrbuch* 23 (1961), 68ff.; P. Bloch, "Nachwirkungen des alten Bundes in der christlichen Kunst," *Monumenta Judaica, Handbuch* (Cologne, 1963), 760ff.; D. Mouriki-Charalambous, "The Octateuch Miniatures of the Byzantine Manuscripts of Cosmas Indicopleustes," Unpublished Ph.D. dissertation, Princeton University, 1970, 112-134; G. Cames, *Allegories et symboles dans l'Hortus Deliciarum* (Leiden, 1971), 21-29. On the Tabernacle as the

typus ecclesiae, cf. J. E. Gaehde, "Carolingian Interpretations of an Early Christian Picture Cycle to the Octateuch in the Bible of San Paolo Fuori Le Mura in Rome," *Frühmittelalterliche Studien* 8 (1974), 364.

23. Acc. No. 30.75, Freer Gallery of Art, Washington, D.C. I am greatly indebted to Prof. Richard Ettinghausen for calling this miniature to my attention. Cf. R. Ettinghausen, "Automata: Islam," *Encyclopedia of World Art* II (New York, 1960), 185-86, plate 77; F. Rosenthal, "A Note on the Mandīl," *Four Essays on Art and Literature in Islam* (Leiden, 1971), 82.

24. This manuscript and Nos. 2-6 (footnote 6), which are related to it, may come from the Catalonian region. They are all described in Metzger, *op. cit.*, 397ff.

25. Nos. 7-12 (note 6) are all related and probably relied on an archetype. Nos. 7 and 10 have the same spaghetti-like formation of the mound with the small tree on top. Nos. 8, 9, 11 are closely related. Especially noteworthy is the altar of burnt offerings with the fleshhooks stuck on the steps of the altar and the tree and mound in the lower left-hand corner of the folio. For the other manuscripts, cf. Metzger, *op. cit.*, 167ff.
No. 14 (note 6). The Temple objects in masoretic micrography may have been added later. Cf. fol. 214 where the masoretic decoration actually runs into the text placed around the folio border.
No. 17 has only one page. The base of the menorah recalls the first iconographic type. The rest of the menorah is related to Nos. 14 and 19. The wide border frame with inscriptions is also found in No. 19. Cf. also No. 16.
It should be noted that no lamps for the oil are found on the menorah and censer-like objects are suspended from the menorah in Nos. 5, 15, 18. Both the snuffers and firepans are

called *mahtah* in the Bible, but Maimonides and other commentators distinguish the two implements by claiming that one served to carry hot coals and that the other was a small vessel into which the ashes of the menorah were placed. Cf. the Hebrew explanation under the censer-like object in No. 15 (p. 182), which appears to follow Rashi's commentary to Ex. 25.38. Cf. also Maimonides, *op. cit.*, VI, 3.4 and *Mishnah, Tamid* 3.6,9.

No. 15 (p. 187) also introduces a mortar, *makhtesh*, (cf. also Nos. 8, 9, 13), into which the ingredients for the incense were placed and compounded. The accompanying inscription again seems to follow Rashi's commentary to Ex. 30.34. Cf. Maimonides, *op. cit.*, II, 2.7.

26. No. 15 introduces five musical instruments on p. 186. No. 14 has a harp on fol. 216. Cf. Maimonides, *op. cit.*, II, 3.4 and *Mishnah, Sukkah* 5.4. Metzger, *op. cit.*, 185, 191.

27. No. 15 (p. 186) and No. 16 (p. 6) show a building. Metzger, *op. cit.*, 188, 191.

28. No. 18 (fol. 4); Metzger, *op. cit.*, 194.

29. Nos. 15 (p. 187) and 18 (fol. 3v). No. 16 has three trees and No. 19 has two trees.

30. *Targum* to Song of Songs 8.5; *Pesikta Rabbati* 31 (Vienna, 1880 ed.), 147a; *Yalkut Shimoni*, Isaiah, Chap. 49, par. 469. Cf. also *Bet ha-Midrash,* ed. A. Jellinek V (Leipzig, 1873), 128 and *Avodat ha-Kodesh* (Warsaw, 1883 ed.), Chap. 40, 108. Cf. a seventh-century poem by Kalir in P. Goodman, *Sukkot and Simhat Torah Anthology* (Philadelphia, 1973), 81-82 and 241. Cf. H. Riesenfeld, "The Resurrection in Ezekiel XXXVII and in the Dura-Europos Paintings," in *No Graven Images,* ed. J. Gutmann (New York, 1971), 144-155; J. B. Curtis, "An Investigation of the Mount of Olives in the Judeo-Christian

Tradition," *Hebrew Union College Annual* 28 (1957), 170-77. As the Passion and Ascension of Jesus occurred on the Mt. of Olives, it was of importance to the Christian tradition. Cf. "Ölberg," *Lexikon der christlichen Ikonographie* III (Freiburg, 1971), 342-49 and G. Kretschmar, "Festkalender und Memorialstätten Jerusalems in altkirchlicher Zeit," *Zeitschrift des Deutschen Palästina Vereins* 87 (1971), 183ff. Cf. also the resurrection of the dead at the Mt. of Olives in the Muslim tradition. J. W. Hirschberg, "The Sources of Moslem Traditions concerning Jerusalem," *Rocznik Orientalistyczny* 7 (1951-52), 343-47.

31. Maimonides, *op. cit.*, I, 6.5 and *Mishnah, Middot* 2.4 and *Parah* 3.6-7.

32. Z. Ameisenowa, "The Tree of Life in Jewish Iconography," *Journal of the Warburg and Courtauld Institutes* 2 (1938-39), 341ff. gives an interpretation of this scene, but fails to see the connection between the Mount of Olives and the cult objects of the Messianic Temple. It is doubtful that the Tree of Life is represented here, as some miniatures show more than one tree (see note 29). An olive tree or trees are no doubt shown so that the Mount of Olives could be more readily identified as a symbol. Most curious is Metzger's criticism of my earlier study, "When the Kingdom Comes: Messianic Themes in Medieval Jewish Art," *Art Journal* 27 (1967-68), 172. While she rejects my theory on *op. cit.*, 402, she readily accepts it as her own on *ibid.*, 201ff.

33. *Mikdashiyah* was already in use in Spain in 1335. Whether the date of the Jerusalem codex is to be read as 1322 or 1422 is uncertain. Cf. Ben-Zvi, *op. cit.*, 366-68 and N. Wieder, "'Sanctuary' as a Metaphor for Scripture," *The Journal of Jewish Social Studies* 8 (1957), 169-73. Cf. also J. N. Hillgarth

and B. Narkiss, "A List of Hebrew Books (1330) and a Contract to Illuminate Manuscripts from Majorca," *Revue des études juives* 120 (1961), 319-20. The designation *mikdashiyah* is found in the Farhi Bible, No. 15 (note 6), pages 1-2 and Kings I (No. 18), fol. 2v.

CONTRIBUTORS

JEAN OUELLETTE, Associate Professor of Bible and Semitic Languages, Université de Montréal. Author of "The Temple of Solomon: A Philological and Archaeological Study" (Ph.D. diss., Hebrew Union College-Jewish Institute of Religion, 1966).

STANLEY FERBER, Professor of Art History, State University of New York at Binghamton. Author of "Crucifixion Iconography in a Group of Ivory Plaques of the Liuthard and Metz Schools" (Ph.D. diss., New York University, 1963).

WALTER CAHN, Associate Professor of the History of Art, Yale University. Author of "The Souvigny Bible: A Study in Romanesque Bible Illumination" (Ph.D. diss., New York University, 1967), *The Romanesque Wooden Doors of Auvergne* (1975).

PRISCILLA SOUCEK, Assistant Professor of the History of Art, University of Michigan. Author of "Illustrated Manuscripts of Nizami's Khamseh: 1386-1482" (Ph.D. diss., New York University, 1971).

JOSEPH GUTMANN, Professor of Art and Art History, Wayne State University. Author of *Jewish Ceremonial Art* (1964), *Beauty in Holiness* (1970), *No Graven Images* (1971), *The Dura-Europos Synagogue* (1973), *The Synagogue* (1975), *Moses Jacob Ezekiel* (1975).

SELECTED BIBLIOGRAPHY ON THE TEMPLE OF SOLOMON

Bloch, P. "Siebenarmige Leuchter in christlichen Kirchen," *Wallraf-Richartz Jahrbuch* 23 (1961).

―――. "Nachwirkungen des alten Bundes in der christlichen Kunst," *Monumenta Judaica*, Handbuch, ed. K. Schilling. Cologne, 1963.

Busink, Th. A. *Der Tempel von Jerusalem*. Leiden, 1970. Reviews by G. Krautwurst, *Zeitschrift des deutschen Palästina-Vereins* 88 (1972), 91-98; H. Weidhaas, *Anatolica* 4 (1972), 184-92; H. Bardtke, *Theologische Literaturzeitung* 97 (1972), 802-10; A. Parrot, *Bibliotheca Orientalis* 30 (1973), 79-84.

Blunt, A. "The Temple of Solomon with Special Reference to South Italian Baroque Art," *Kunsthistorische Forschungen. Otto Pächt zu seinem 70. Geburtstag*. Salzburg, 1972.

De la Ruffinière du Prey, P. "Solomonic Symbolism in Borrominis Church of S. Ivo alla Sapienza," *Zeitschrift für Kunstgeschichte* 31 (1968).

Fagiolo, M. "Borromini in Laterano 'il Nuovo Tempio' per il Concilio Universale," *L'Arte* 4 (1971).

Gutmann, J., ed. *No Graven Images: Studies in Art and the Hebrew Bible*. New York, 1971.

―――. "The History of the Ark," *Zeitschrift für die alttestamentliche Wissenschaft* 83 (1971).

―――. "When the Kingdom Comes: Messianic Themes in Medieval Jewish Art," *Art Journal* 27 (1967-68).

Haussherr, R. "Templum Salomonis und Ecclesia Christi, zu einem Bildvergleich der Bible moralisée," *Zeitschrift für Kunstgeschichte* 31 (1968).

Hermann, W. "Unknown Designs for the 'Temple of Jerusalem' by Claude Perrault," *Essays in the History of Architecture presented to Rudolf Wittkower*. London, 1967.

Hirschberg, J. W. "The Sources of Moslem Traditions concerning Jerusalem," *Rocznik Orientalistyczny* 17 (1951-52).

Kenyon, K. "New Evidence on Solomon's Temple," *Mélanges de l'Université Saint-Joseph* 46 (1970).

Krinsky, C. H. "Representations of the Temple of Jerusalem before 1500," *Journal of the Warburg and Courtauld Institutes* 33 (1970).

Metzger, T. "Les objets du culte, le sanctuaire du désert et le Temple de Jérusalem dans les bibles hebraïques médiévales enluminées, en Orient et en Espagne," *Bulletin of the John Rylands Library* 52-53 (1970).

Ouellette, J. "The Temple of Solomon: A Philological and Archaeological Study." Unpublished Ph.D. dissertation, Hebrew Union College-Jewish Institute of Religion. Cincinnati, 1966.

_____. "The Yāṣīa' and the Ṣelā'ōt: Two Mysterious Structures in Solomon's Temple," *Journal of Near Eastern Studies* 31 (1972).

_____. "The Solomonic Debîr according to the Hebrew Text of I Kings 6," *Journal of Biblical Literature* 89 (1970).

_____. "Le vestibule du Temple de Salomon, était-il un bit ḥilâni?" *Revue biblique* 76 (1969).

SELECTED BIBLIOGRAPHY

Parrot, A. *The Temple of Jerusalem.* New York, 1955.

Rupprecht, K. "Nachrichtungen von Erweiterungen und Renovierung des Tempels in I Könige 6," *Zeitschrift des deutschen Palästina-Vereins* 88 (1972).

Rosenau, H. "Jacob Judah Leon Templo's Contribution to Architectural Imagery," *Journal of Jewish Studies* 23 (1972).

──────. "A Note on the Reconstruction of Solomon's Temple and Palace by Louis Maillet," *Gazette des Beaux-Arts* 78 (1971).

──────. "The Architecture of Nicolaus de Lyra's Temple Illustrations and the Jewish Tradition," *Journal of Jewish Studies* 25 (1974).

Salzberger, G. *Salomos Tempelbau und Thron in der semitischen Sagenliteratur.* Berlin, 1912.

Scheja, G. "Hagia Sophia und Templum Salomonis," *Istanbuler Mitteilungen* 12 (1962).

Taylor, R. "El Padre Villalpando y sus ideas estéticas," *Academia, Anales y Boletin de la Real Academia de San Fernando.* Madrid, 1952.

Vajda, G. "La description du Temple de Jérusalem d'après le K. al-masālik wal-mamālik d'al Muhallabi: ses éléments bibliques et rabbiniques," *Journal Asiatique* 247 (1959).

Vincent, L.-H. and Steve, A. M., *Jérusalem de l'Ancien Testament.* Paris, 1956.

INDEX

Aaron, 29
'Abd al-Malik, 45, 93-96
Abraham, VIII, 80, 101, 104
Abū Bakr, 101-02, 107
Abū Maryan, 89
Abū Ṭalib, 107
Adam, 29
Aharoni, Yohanan, 5
'Ā'isha, 106
Aix-en-Provence, cloister, 55
Albright, William, 7
Alexander the Great, 74-75
Alexandria, 30, 37, 83
Apocrypha, 29
Aqsa Mosque, 45, 47, 48, 54, 55, 73, 100, 104
Arad, 4, 5, 9
Ark of the Covenant, 26, 31, 126

Babylonian Talmud:
   Eruvin 57b, 18 n. 40
   Horayot 12a, 141 n. 12
   Shevuot 20b, 139 n. 10
   Yoma 21b, 39b, 119 n. 87; *52b, 54a*, 141 n. 21
al-Balādhurī, 78
Baldwin V, 54
Barnett, Richard, 9
Bayt al-Muqaddas, 77, 78, 80, 91, 101, 102, 109, 111
Benjamin of Tudela, 68 n. 29
Berlin, Staatsbibliothek: Theol. lat. fol. 485 (Itala), 24, 38
Bethlehem, 25
Beth Shearim, 37
Bezalel, 22, 33, 34, 57, 69 n. 33

Biblical figures:
  Aaron, 29
  Abraham, VIII, 80, 101, 104
  Adam, 29
  Bezalel, 22, 33, 34, 57, 69 n. 33
  David, 33, 34, 47, 53, 80, 81, 82, 89
  Hiram, 24-26
  Isaac, 80
  Ishmael, VIII
  Jacob, 47, 80, 82
  Moses, 29, 101
  Zerubbabel, 22
Bît ḫilâni, 8, 11
al-Bīrūnī, 74-77, 93
Bukhtnaṣṣar *see* Nebuchadnezzar
Busink, Theodor, 3, 5, 11

Cassiodorus, 28, 30, 35
Champeix, Auvergne, church of, 63 n. 14
Charlemange, VIII, 70 n. 33
Cherubim, 26, 126, 131, 139 n. 9
Christ, 47, 53, 75, 89, 101, 144 n. 30
II Chronicles 3, 1, 10, 14-15 n. 14
Churches: St. John of Studion, Constantinople, 22; S. Maria Maggiore, Rome, 25; Moissac, cloister, 50; Würzburg, cathedral, 51; Sant' Agostino, Andria, 52; Holy Apostles, Constantinople, 53; Spaleto, Duomo, 54; Aix-en-Provence, 55; St. Lazare, Avallon, 55; St. Peter's, Rome, 55-56, 67 n. 29; Essen Minster, 56; Champeix, Auvergne, 63 n. 14; S. Maria Maggiore, Tuscania, 52
Clement of Alexandria, 52-53
Codex Amiatinus, 24, 27, 30, 35-38, 128
Constantine, 55, 89
Constantinople, 92-93

Crucifixion, 49, 89, 95
Crusaders, VII, 46, 48, 50, 54

Darmstadt, Hessisches Landesmuseum, 53
David, 33, 34, 47, 53, 80, 81, 82, 89
Demons, Solomon control of, 83, 84, 86
Deuteronomy 5, 126-27; *22*, 12 n. 3
Devir, 4, 6, 128
Dhorme, Edouard, 2
al-Dīnawarī, 85-86
Dome of the Rock, VII, 45, 47, 48, 54, 73, 76, 79, 94, 95, 99, 103, 108
Domus Sapientiae, 50
Dura-Europos, synagogue, 125
Durandus of Mende, 50

Edinburgh, University Library: Ms. No. 161 (al-Bīrūnī), 76-77
Essen Minster, 56
Eusebius, 22, 23
Evangelists, portraits of, 52
Exodus 20, 126-27; *25*, 28, 126; *26*, 31; *27*, 127; *30*, 127; *31*, 24; *37-40*, 127
Ezekiel 40-41, 8, 12 n. 3

ibn al-Faqīh, 80, 82, 85
Florence, Bibl. Laurentiana: Amiatinus 1 (Codex Amiatinus)
Frankfort, Henri, 10
Frederick II of Prussia, VIII

Gabriel, 101
Gregory III, 55

Ḥamd Allah Mustawfī, 103
Hamza Isfahānī, 74-75
Ḥasan al-Basrī, 101

Hazor, 4, 6, 11
Hekhal, 6, 10
Heliopolis, 19 n. 44
Hermann of Lobdeburg, 51
Herodotus, 9
Hiram, 24-26
Holy Apostles, Constantinople, 53
Holy Sepulchre, 45, 49
Honorius of Autun, 49-50

ibn Isḥāq, 101
Iconostasis, 53
Idalion, 9
Inscriptions, 25, 52, 63 n. 14
Isaac, 80
Istanbul, Topkapi Sarayi Müzesi: Hazine 1654 (Rashīd al-Dīn), 84; Hazine 2154, 103; Karaite Synagogue: Pentateuch, 130
Ishmael, VIII

Jacob, 47, 80, 82
Jalāl al-Dīn Rūmī, 104, 109
James I of England, VIII
James of Kokkinobaphos, 53
al-Jazarī, 130
Jerusalem, map of, 46
John of Capgrave, 67 n. 29
John of Würzburg, 51
John the Grammarian, 33-34
Josephus Flavius, 30, 41
Justinian I, VIII, 53, 69 n. 33

I Kings 6-7, VII, 1-7, 10, 11, 24, 28, 128

II Kings 22, 12 n. 3
Koran: *Sura 5*, 113 n. 20; *Sura 17*, 91, 99-100, 105, 107; *Sura 21*, 79, 83, 98; *Sura 34*, 83, 86; *Sura 38*, 90-91
Krinsky, Carol, 46

Latin Kingdom, 46, 55
Layard, Henry A., 9
Levis, 131
Leviticus 24-25, 126-27
London, British Museum: Ms. Add. 32343 (Map of Jerusalem), 46
Lucian, 19 n. 44
Luke 21:5-6, 130

Maimonides, 128-29, 140-41
Mark 13:1-2, 130
Masjid al-Aqṣa see Aqsa Mosque
al-Masjid see *Bayt al-Muqaddas*
Mass, 54
al-Masʿūdī, 74
Matthew 24:1-2, 130
Mekka, 83, 91, 99-101, 105-08
Mélathron (architrave), 7
Melodia (personification), 53
Menorah (lampstand), 31-32, 34, 126
Messiah, 87, 129
Miḥrāb, 83, 89-90
Mikdashiyah, 132, 144-45 n. 33
Mikdash me'at (minor sanctuary), VIII
Milan, Bibl. Ambrosiana; Cod. F 205 Inf. (Iliad), 24-27
Mishnah:
   Middot 2:4, 132
   Menahot 11:5-6, 140 n. 13

Sukkah 5:4, 140 n. 26
Tamid 2:5, 3:9, 140 nn. 12-13, 143 n. 25
Yoma 2:1, 2:5, 140 nn. 12-13
Zebahim 9:7, 140 n. 13
Mishneh Torah *see* Maimonides
Moissac, cloister of, 50
Molten Sea, 56, 58
Moses, 29, 101
Mount Athos, Psalter, 33, 36
Mount Moriah, 45, 73, 91, 94, 103
Mount of Olives (*har ha-zeitim*), 131-32, 143-44 n. 30
al-Muhallabī, 82, 87, 89, 96
Muhammad, Night Journey (*Isrā'*), 73, 91, 95, 99, 102, 105; Ascension (*Mi'rāj*), 73, 99; chooses milk, 101, 104
al-Muqaddasī, 98, 102
Musical Instruments *see* Temple

Nebuchadnezzar, 74-78
New Solomonic Temple, VIII, 130
New Testament References:
　Matthew 24:1-2, 130
　Mark 13:1-2, 130
　Luke 21:5-6, 130
Northumbria, 27
Noth, Martin, 2
Numbers 8, 10, 17, 126-27

Octateuchs, 129
Old Testament, Jewish, in Latin, 40 n. 14
Old Testament References:
　Exodus 20, 126-27; *25*, 28, 126; *26*, 31; *27*, 127; *30*, 127; *31*, 34; *37-40*, 127
　Leviticus 24-25, 126-27

Numbers 8, 10, 17, 126-27
Deuteronomy 5, 126-27; *22*, 12 n. 3
II Samuel 24, 81
I Kings 6-7, VII, 1-7, 10, 11, 24, 28, 128
II Kings 22, 12 n. 3
II Chronicles 3, 1, 10, 14-15 n. 14
Zechariah 14, 131
Ezekiel 40-41, 8, 12 n. 3
Psalms 14, 28; *86*, 30; *113*, 33
Proverbs 9, 51

Paris, Bibliothèque Nationale: Ms. lat. 6 (Bible of San Pedro de Roda), 26-27; Ms. gr. 139 (Paris Psalter), 53; Ms. Gr. 1208 (Homilies of James Kokkinobaphos), 53; Ms. supp. turc. 190 (Mi'raj Nāmeh), 102; Ms. hebr. 7 (Perpignan Bible), 126-27; Ms. hebr. 31 (Saragossa Bible), 131
Paulinus, bishop of Tyre, 22
Persepolis, 83
Petrus Mallius, 56
Philip II of Spain, VIII
Pompeian frescoes, 53
Porta aurea, 48, 60 n. 3
Proverbs 9, 51
Prudentius, 23
Psalms 14, 28; *86*, 30; *113*, 33
Quedlinburg Itala, 24, 38
Qur'ān *see* Koran
ibn Qutaybah, 74

Rainier of Huy, 56
Rashi, 143 n. 25
Rashīd al-Dīn, 84

INDEX 157

Redaktionsgeschichte (editorial history), 3
Richard of Saint-Victor, 58
Rupprecht, Konrad, 2, 3, 8

Sabbath, 127
Salah al-Dīn, 49
Samaritan, 31-32, 37-38
St. Peter's, Rome, 55-56, 67 n. 29
II Samuel 24, 81
Samuel ha-Levi Abulafia, 128
Sanctuary vessels, 126-27
Sennacherib, 78
Sheba, queen of, 26
Shofar, 32, 127
Siccardus of Cremona, 49
Solomon ha-Levi ben Bouya'a, 31
Stabula Salomonis (Solomon's stables), 47
Suger, abbot of Saint-Denis, 58
Sulaymān, 93
Sibylline Oracles, 29
Synagogues: Worms, Germany, 63 n. 14; Dura Europos, Syria, 125; El Tránsito, Toledo, Spain, 128

al-Ṭabarī, 77, 79ff., 105-06, 110
Tabernacle, 27-28, 31-38, 43, 125, 128, 133 n. 3
Table of showbread, 34, 126-27
Tell Tainat, Syria, 4-5, 10
Templars, 48-50, 55
Temple, musical instruments of, 131
Temple, dedication of, 24
Temple, destruction of, 75-79
Temple, Messianic, 126ff.

Temple of Wisdom, 23
Temples: Ezekiel's, 1; Tell Tainat, Syria, 4-5, 10; Hazor, 4, 6; Arad, 4-5; Herakles-Melkart, Tyre, 9; Idalion, 9; Atagartis, Heliopolis, 19 n. 44
Templum Domini, 47
Templum Salomonis, 47
Ten Commandments, 126-27, 130-31
Theodorich, 49, 51
Torah ark, 125
Torah case, 31-32, 37
Trees of gold, 87

Überlieferungsgeschichte (study of traditions), 3
Ulam, 5, 6, 8, 10
'Umar ibn al-Khaṭṭāb, 73, 88-89, 90-93
Ummayads, 45, 93-94, 97

Vaux, Roland de, 3
Virgin Mary, 48, 53, 95
Vulgate, 27

Wahb ibn Munabbih, 74, 81, 85, 86, 97
Weitzmann, Kurt, 36
Wright, Ernest, G., 3

Yadin, Yigael, 5-7
Yakhin and Boaz, 7-11, 51, 63 n. 14, 131
Yazīd b. Mu'āwiya, 92
Yeivin, Samuel, 7

Zachariah, annunciation to, 80
Zechariah 14, 131
Zerubbabel, 22, 69 n. 33

THE TEMPLE OF SOLOMON

ILLUSTRATIONS

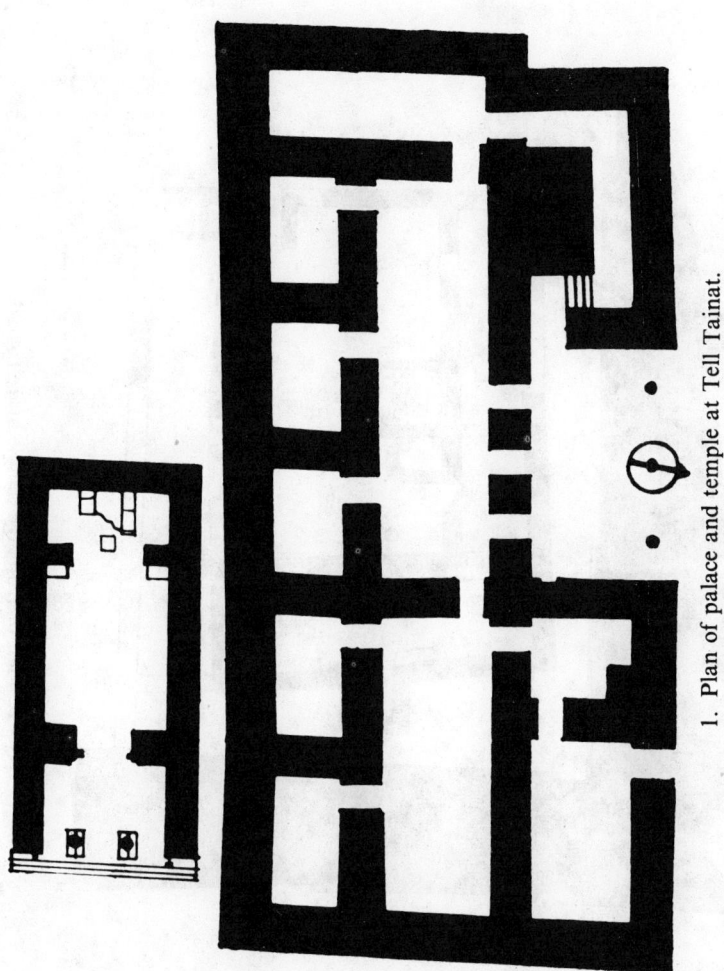

1. Plan of palace and temple at Tell Tainat.

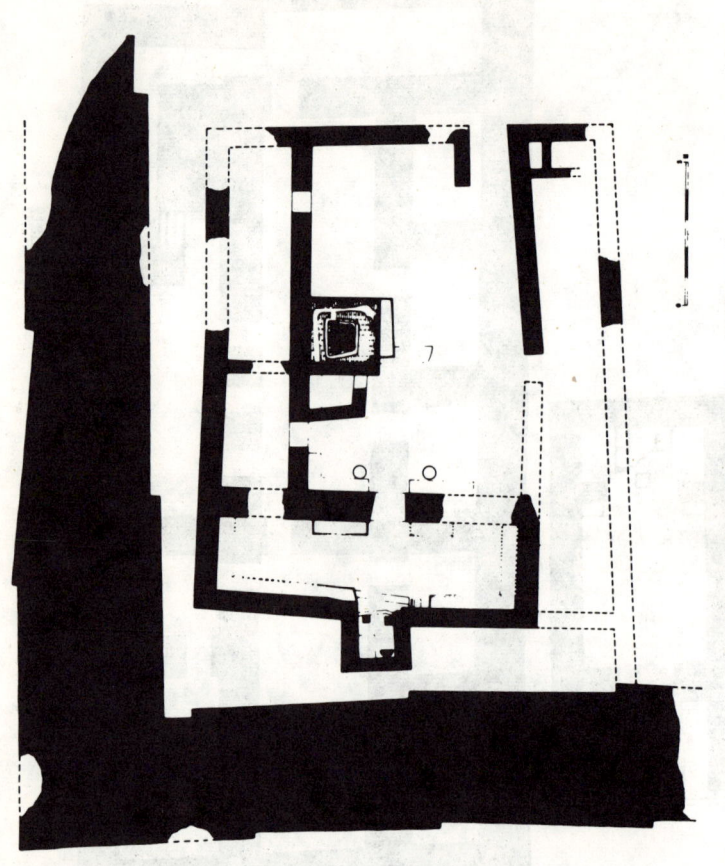

2. Plan of Iron Age temple at Tell Arad.

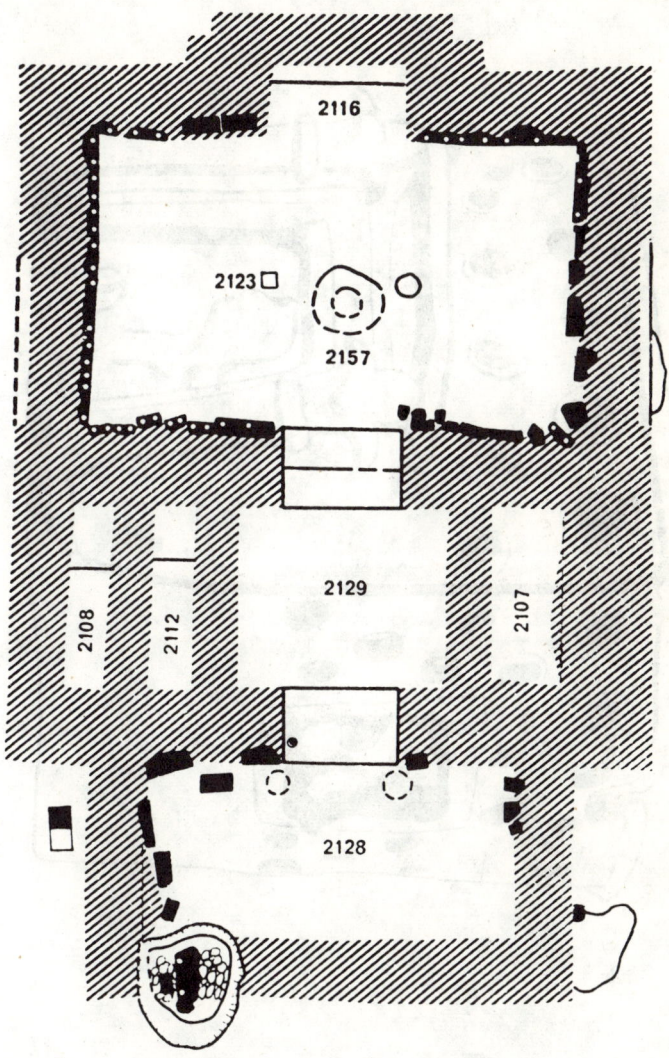

3. Plan of temple at Hazor (Stratum Ib).

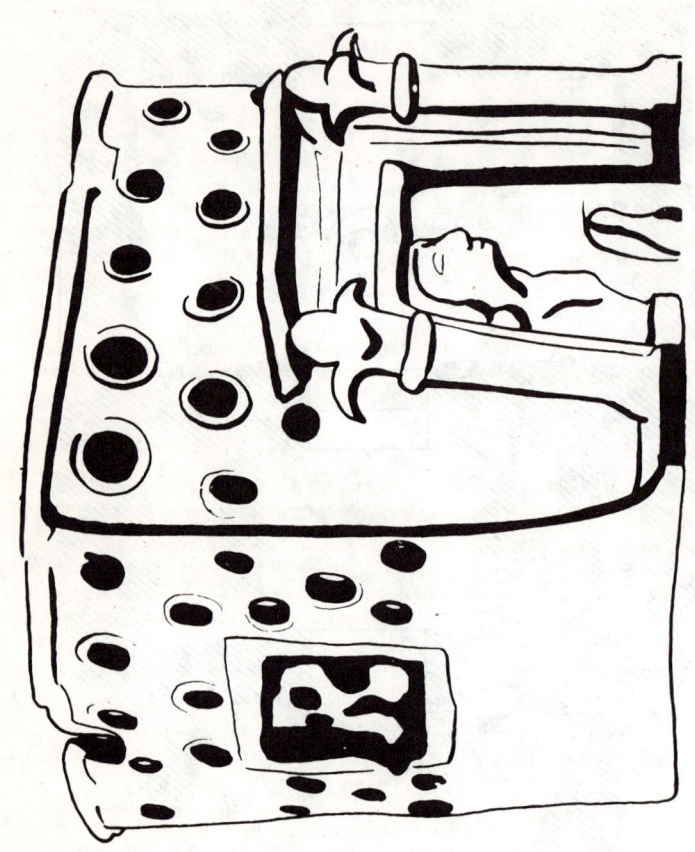

4. Pottery model of small temple from Idalion, Cyprus.

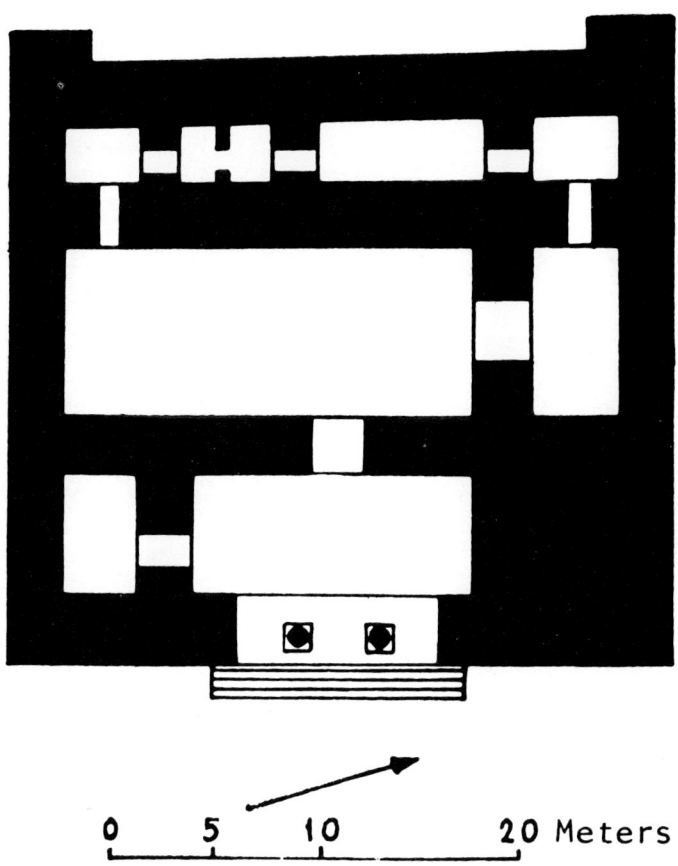

5. Plan of a ḫilâni at Zinçirli.

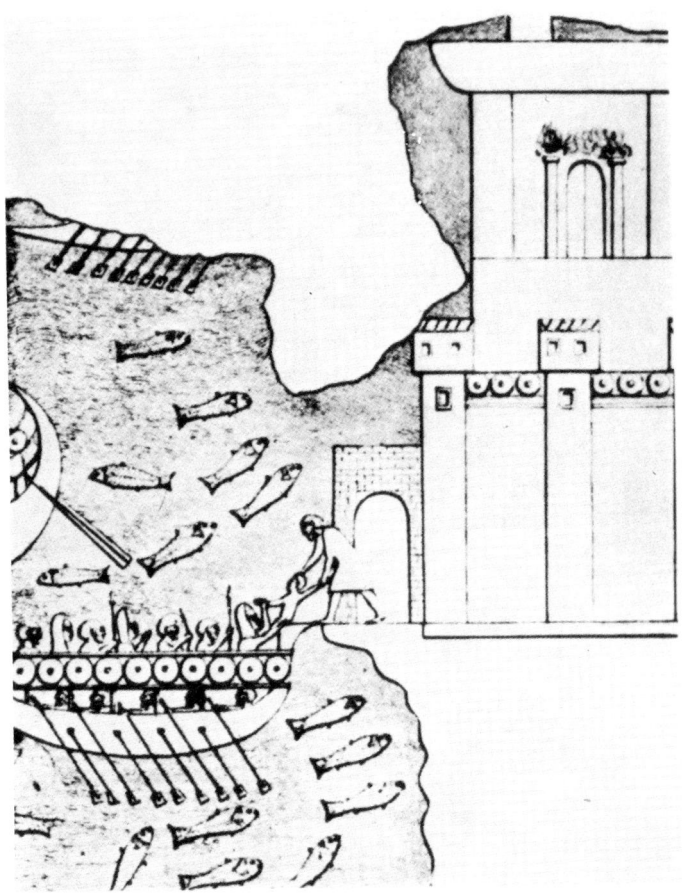

6. Layard's drawing of Assyrian relief from Kouyunjik.

7. "Trojans attacking a walled camp," Milan Iliad, Milan, Bibl. Ambrosiana, Cod. F. 205 Inf.

8. "Bethlehem," Mosaic on Triumphal arch, S. Maria Maggiore, Rome.

9. "Life of Solomon and building the Temple," Bible of San Pedro of Roda, Paris, Bibl. Nationale, lat. Ms. 6, fol. 129v.

10. "Temple in the Wilderness," Codex Amiatinus, Florence, Bibl. Laurentiana, Amiatinus 1, fols. 2v-3.

11. "Tabernacle," First Leningrad Bible, Leningrad, Public Library, Ms. II, 17.

12. Torah case, Samaritan, Samaritan Temple Treasure, Nablus.

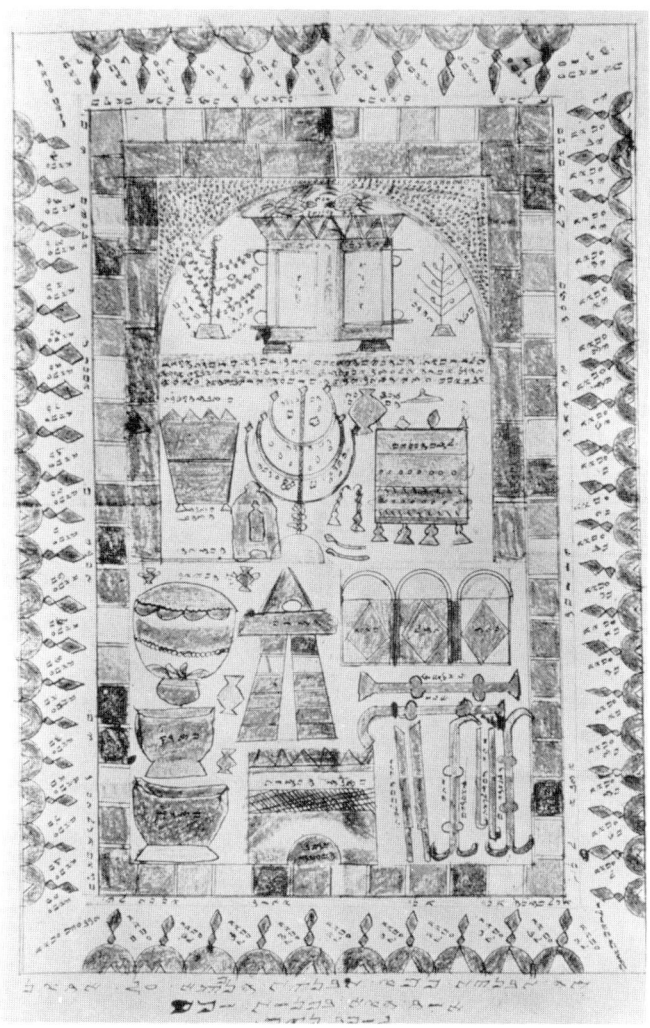

13. "Tabernacle/Temple," Samaritan drawing, location unknown.

14. Illustration to Psalm 113, Mt. Athos Psalter, Mt. Athos, Ms. Patocrator 61, fol. 165.

15. Harām al-Sharīf (Temple precinct), Jerusalem.

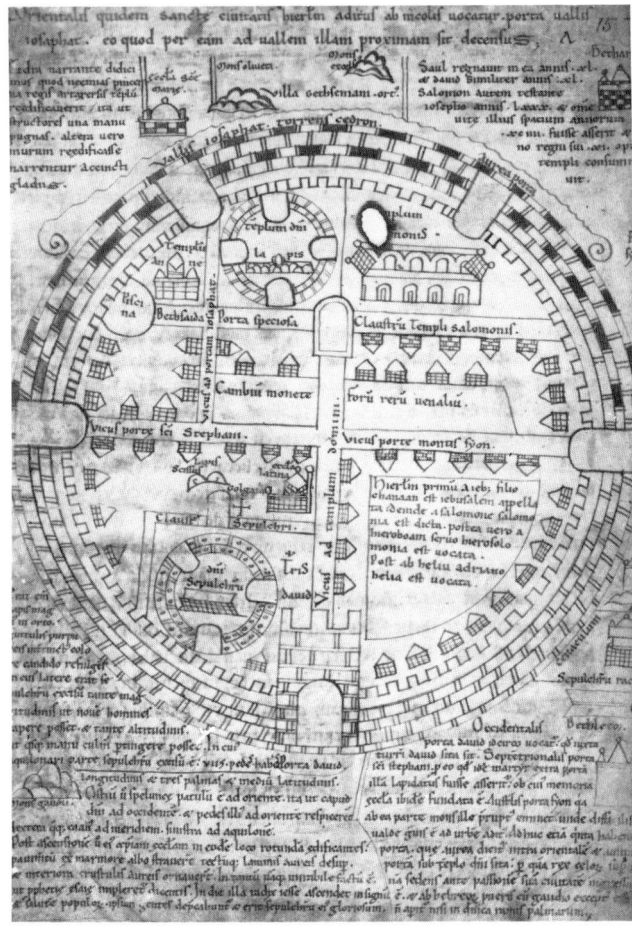

16. "Map of Jerusalem," London, British Museum, Add. 32343, fol. 15.

17. *"Iachim* and *Booz,"* formerly facade, Würzburg Cathedral.

18. Fragment of a knotted column. Darmstadt, Hessisches Landesmuseum.

19. Fragment of a knotted column, Darmstadt, Hessisches Landesmuseum.

20. Central portal of the west facade, Ferrara Cathedral.

21. "David as a shepherd," Paris Psalter, Paris, Bibl. Nationale, Ms. gr. 139, fol. lv.

22. "Ascension," Homilies of James of Kokkinobaphos, Paris, Bibl. Nationale, Ms. gr. 1208, fol. 3v.

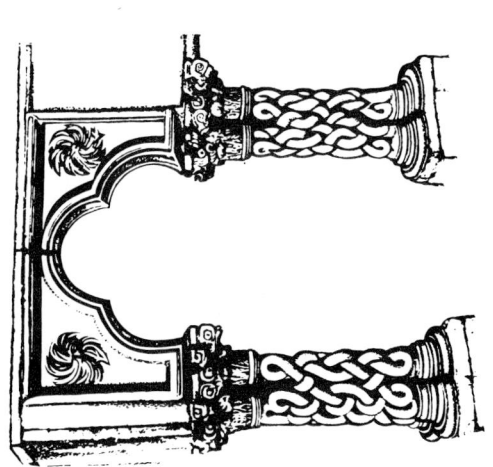

23. Niche, Dome of the Rock, Jerusalem (left). Tomb of Baldwin V, after a drawing of Elzear Horn (right).

24. South portal of west facade, St. Lazare, Avallon.

25. "Bukhtnassar orders the destruction of the Temple," Al-Bīrūnī, Āthār al-Bāqiya, Edinburgh University Library, Ms. No. 161, fol. 134v.

26. "Solomon deludes the demons into finishing the Temple," Rashīd al-Dīn, *Jāmiʿ al-Tawārīkh*, Istanbul, Topkapi Sarayi Müzesi Kütüphanesi, Hazine 1654, fol. 18v.

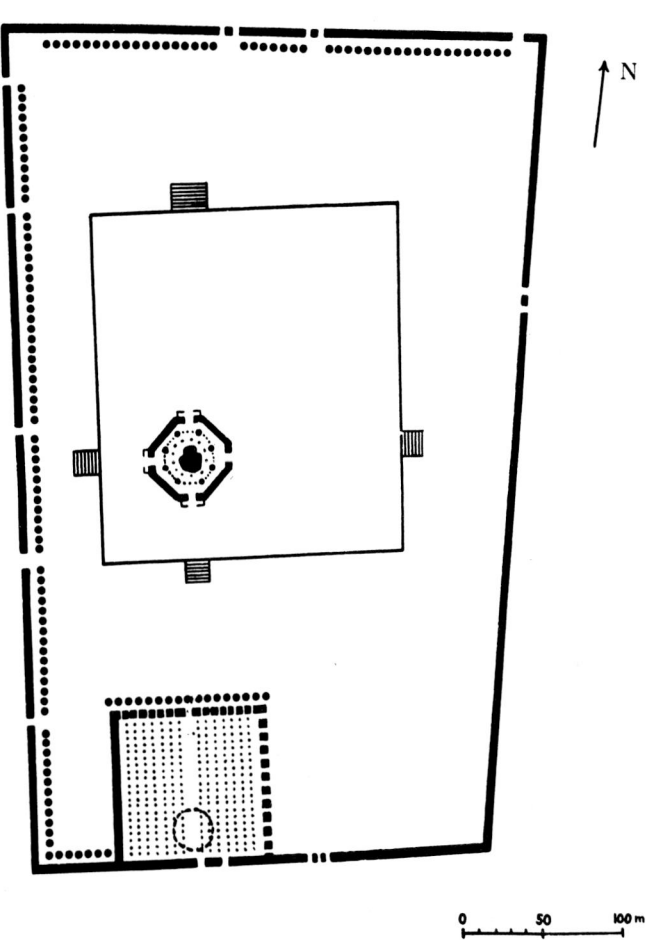

27. Sketch plan of Harām al-Sharīf with Dome of the Rock and Masjid al-Aqṣā.

28. Tree with jeweled trunk from a pier of the octagonal arcade, Dome of the Rock, Jerusalem.

29. Composite plant with jeweled ornaments from a pier of the octagonal arcade, Dome of the Rock, Jerusalem.

30. Plants with crowns and jewels, inner surface of octagonal arcade, Dome of the Rock, Jerusalem.

31. "The Prophet Muhammad leads other Prophets in prayer on his visit to Masjid al-Aqṣā," *Mi'rāj Nāmeh*, Paris, Bibl. Nationale, Suppl. turc 190, fol. 7.

32. "The Prophet Muhammad chooses milk in Masjid al-Aqṣā," Istanbul, Topkapi Sarayi Müzesi Kütüphanesi, Hazine 2154, fol. 62.

33. "The Prophet's vision of Masjid al-Aqṣā during the discussion with Abū Bakr, "Istanbul, Topkapi Sarayi Müzesi Kütüphanesi, Hazine 2154, fol. 107.

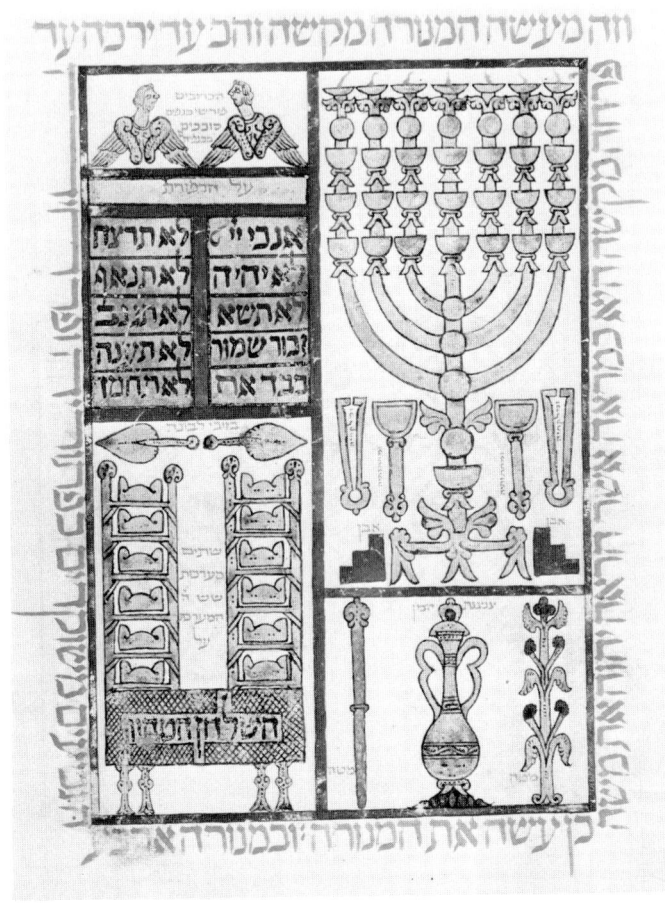

34. "Sanctuary vessels," Bible, Paris, Bibl. Nationale, Ms. hebr. 7, fol. 12v.

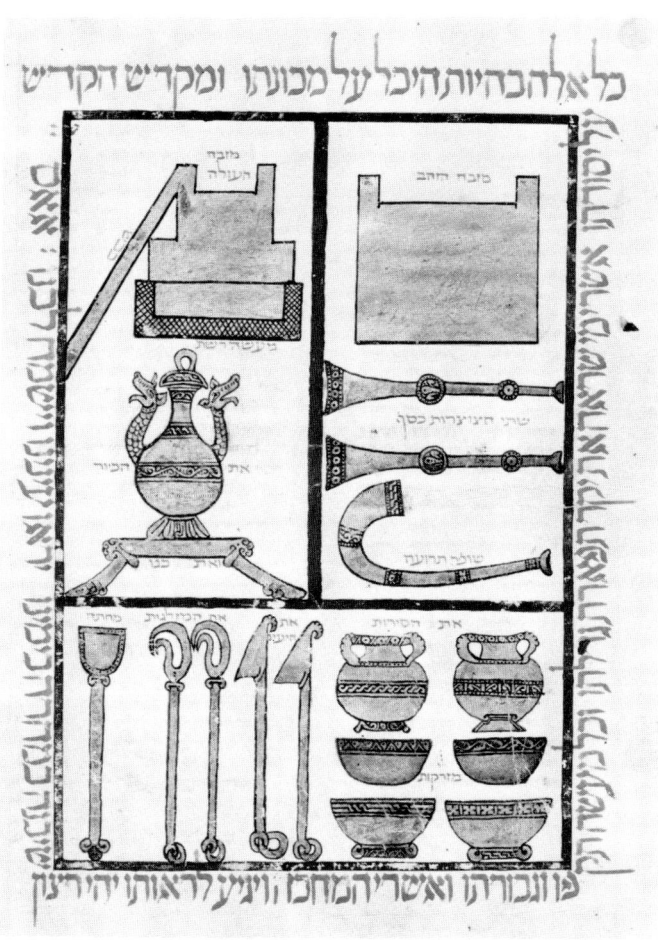

35. "Sanctuary vessels," Bible, Paris, Bibl. Nationale, Ms. hebr. 7, fol. 13.

36. Handwashing device, al-Jazarī, *Treatise on Automata*, Washington, Freer Gallery of Art, Acc. No. 30.75.

37. "Sanctuary vessels," Pentateuch, Istanbul, Karaite synagogue, p. 18.

38. "Sanctuary vessels," Pentateuch, Istanbul, Karaite synagogue, p. 19.

39. "Mount of Olives," Bible, Paris, Bibl. Nationale, Ms. hebr. 31, fol. 4.